With Best Wishes

Arpad

The Online Trading Cookbook

For other titles in the Wiley Trading Series
please see www.wiley.com/finance

THE ONLINE TRADING COOKBOOK

Alpesh B. Patel
Paresh H. Kiri

A John Wiley & Sons, Ltd., Publication

Registered office
John Wiley & Sons Ltd, The Atrium, Southern Gate, Chichester, West Sussex, PO19 8SQ, United Kingdom

For details of our global editorial offices, for customer services and for information about how to apply for permission to reuse the copyright material in this book please see our website at www.wiley.com.

Library of Congress Cataloging-in-Publication Data

Patel, Alpesh B.
   The online trading cookbook / Alpesh Patel, Paresh Kiri.
     p. cm. – (Wiley trading series)
   Includes bibliographical references and index.
   ISBN 978-0-470-68445-0 (cloth)
1. Electronic trading of securities.   2. Investments–Computer network resources.   I. Kiri, Paresh.   II. Title.
   HG4515.95.P277   2012
   332.640285′4678–dc23

                                 2012004086

A catalogue record for this book is available from the British Library.

ISBN 978-0-470-68445-0 (hardback) ISBN 978-0-470-66246-5 (ebk)
ISBN 978-0-470-66182-6 (ebk)   ISBN 978-0-470-66171-0 (ebk)

Set in 10/12pt Times by Aptara Inc., New Delhi, India.
Printed and bound in Great Britain by TJ International Ltd, Padstow, Cornwall, UK

Alpesh Patel Dedication

In memory of Sushilabhen R. Patel

> Still your mind in me, still yourself in me, and without a doubt you shall
> be united with me, Lord of Love, dwelling in your heart

(Bhagavad Gita)

Paresh Kiri Dedication

Who better to dedicate my first book than the most important people in my life? The saying 'behind every great man is a great woman' should maybe read, 'Behind every great man is an even *greater* woman'.

To the two greater than I women in my life – now and forever – my wife – Rajee Kiri, and H.H. Shri Mataji Nirmala Devi, simply known to us as MOTHER.

Not forgetting the children, Mihir, Angelee and Shivam.

And finally, Alpesh B. Patel, a staunch advocate for justice and fairness.

Contents

PART III   AMUSE-BOUCHE

PART IV   ENTREMET

PART V   ENTREE

PART VI   MAIN

PART VII   DESSERT

PART VIII   PANTRY

Preface

A LIVING BOOK

We want readers of this book to engage with us as authors, therefore we have provided a Facebook page, a Twitter page, a blog with the latest trading ideas based on our strategies, our monthly market analysis newsletter (about 50 pages each month) and links to our online education, as well as our email at the end of this preface. We genuinely want to have an ongoing teaching relationship with all our readers.

A few years ago Alpesh won a competition in the *Financial Times*. He correctly forecast the value of the FTSE 100, the UK's main equity index, over a 12-month period. He came within 0.5% of the final value. That was closer than his competitors, who included traders, brokers, analysts, FT journalists and the editor's cat. Some were out by as much as 50%. These were clever people. They were market experts and specialists. Alpesh is one of you, dear reader. Someone who knows they can do it themselves.

> Our aims with this book are: to teach our own and others' successful strategies; to make this the only trading book you will ever need; to use social networks and YouTube to ensure a critical focus on what troubles and what interests you.

The aims of this book are: to teach our own and others' successful strategies; to make this the only trading book you will ever need; to use social networks and YouTube to ensure a critical focus on what troubles and what interests you. We would then suggest that you use Alpesh's weekly appearances on the BBC to double-check what the private investor/trader wants and needs to know. From our experience we realise that it is important to spend some time explaining 'what the rich and successful traders do' in simple terms. Too often expert authors forget that unless the reader 'gets it' the whole exercise and satisfaction of a book become redundant.

This book covers some of the techniques used, why we can't rely on 'experts' and why we should learn to invest ourselves, how trading can be straightforward and, most importantly, how we can do it. These are no-nonsense recipes for trading success from cordon-bleu traders.

A three-sentence summary of the book would be as follows. The cookbook format is one of the most enduring and popular for teaching complicated skills. Trading skills can be learnt and presented as simple recipes. This book provides exactly that from trading strategies to risk and money management.

My essential pitch to you, dear reader, is that this format has never been used. Each recipe presents as ingredients what the trader needs to do, the tools and the preparation. And then illustrates successful examples, and some that didn't work and why. Both the proven format and its simplicity are compelling and unique in their application to trading.

The book is divided into sections appropriately aimed at the novice, intermediate and advanced trader, thereby enabling beginners to learn how to trade or, in the case of advanced traders, to become better traders. The strategies are ranked according to complexity.

So why not simply have one or two strategies? Because, like recipes, traders use different strategies for different purposes. If you want to have a portfolio of short-term and long-term trades, or ones based on equities and others for forex, then you need different recipes. But why different time frames and different asset classes (like stocks and bonds)? Because as the intermediate and advanced trader will tell you, this diversifies your risk and ensures there is always capital working for you.

By having more than one strategy, for example investment A and investment B, the risk is reduced, because the combination of both can smooth out your returns.

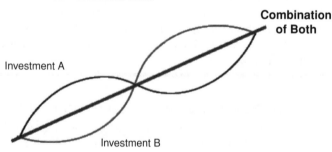

**Combining two investments
that move in opposite directions
can eliminate risk.**

Combination
of Both

Investment A

Investment B

This book will help readers:

1. improve their profitability as traders
2. learn the skills needed to trade
3. save time and money by providing specific focused strategies

BUT WHO SAYS WE'RE ANY GOOD?

We've taken three approaches with the strategies in this book. First, we've used personal practical experience. Second, we've back-tested. For instance the illustration below shows how we tested a multitude of strategies over different time frames.

Strategy		Long	Short	Total	Total	%Total	Long	Short	Profit Factor	Avg Dur (in days)	Sharpe	%Max DD
11) BuyAndHold		1	0	1	4.65k	4.65	4.65k	0.00	0.00	1822.00	0.09	56.52
12) Boll		9	9	18	-1.72k	-1.72	-92.59	-1.63k	0.97	98.83	0.03	49.66
13) CMCI		27	27	54	-37.00k	-37.00	-12.50k	-24.50k	0.60	33.70	-0.34	54.19
14) DMI		52	52	104	12.58k	12.58	20.36k	-7.78k	1.12	17.45	0.13	33.04
15) MACD		53	53	106	13.26k	13.26	18.84k	-5.58k	1.10	17.08	0.15	19.28
16) RSI		3	4	7	-32.98k	-32.98	-18.70k	-14.28k	0.39	246.57	-0.28	52.12
17) TAS		27	27	54	-17.91k	-17.91	-800.57	-17.11k	0.81	33.59	-0.13	43.92
18) Wm		27	27	54	-53.40k	-53.40	-23.57k	-29.83k	0.43	33.65	-0.57	59.62
19) PTPS		63	63	126	-54.35k	-54.35	-22.57k	-31.78k	0.60	14.39	-0.63	57.04
20) SMAvg		43	43	86	812.01	0.81	9.23k	-8.42k	1.01	21.19	0.02	28.73
21) EMAvg		46	46	92	38.19k	38.19	35.22k	2.97k	1.40	19.75	0.36	29.81
22) WMAvg		58	58	116	-27.32k	-27.32	-8.08k	-19.24k	0.78	15.64	-0.31	37.82
23) VMAvg		80	80	160	-40.48k	-40.48	-14.44k	-26.04k	0.71	11.34	-0.46	53.00
24) TMAvg		40	40	80	22.79k	22.79	23.46k	-673.50	1.22	22.77	0.23	17.23
25) ADOsc		343	342	685	-63.97k	-63.97	-27.37k	-36.59k	0.71	2.66	-0.79	73.10
26) GOC		22	23	45	21.93k	21.93	22.50k	-568.38	1.22	40.13	0.22	24.22
27) KBand		37	37	74	8.87k	8.87	10.72k	-1.85k	1.06	24.50	0.12	34.87
28) MAE		14	13	27	8.39k	8.39	6.38k	2.00k	1.09	58.67	0.12	38.53
29) MAO		72	72	144	-22.95k	-22.95	-5.21k	-17.74k	0.84	12.60	-0.20	41.20
30) Fear & Greed		53	53	106	-15.43k	-15.43	643.71	-16.08k	0.88	17.10	-0.14	41.51
31) Rex		249	248	497	-81.21k	-81.21	-40.45k	-40.76k	0.57	3.67	-1.26	83.29

Third, some of the strategies are our trading software. The performance figures are also displayed in the following table. The software is the 'Alpesh Patel Special Edition of ShareScope' (www.sharescope.co.uk/alpesh).

Alpesh Performance Figures

Year	APSE	FTSE All-Share
2004	+34.9%	+9.2%
2005	+44.2%	+18.1%
2006	+40.6%	+10.8%
2007	−2.3%	+2.3%
2008	−18.4%	−32.4%
2009	+17.4%	+28.0%
2010	+16.1%	+9.1%
Total	**+197.2%**	**+38.0%**
CAGR	**+16.8%**	**+4.7%**

Note: Performance is calculated as the percentage price change between the closing prices of the first and last trading days of the year.
Spread and dealing costs have not been included.
Source: www.sharescope.co.uk/alpesh

We trust you will enjoy the book and that we achieve our aims. Any questions and you can reach us below:

Email: Alpesh.patel@tradermind.com with questions or to sign up to our monthly
    markets newsletter
Facebook: alpeshp1
Twitter: alpeshbp
Blog: www.alpeshblog.com
Forex education and trading: www.alpeshpatel.com
Online education: www.investingbetter.com
Spreadtrading: www.alpeshpatel.com/etx
Trading software: www.sharescope.co.uk/alpesh

Acknowledgements

The neural activity of someone whose investments are making money is indistinguishable from that of someone who is high on cocaine or morphine.

—Jason Zweig

I am indebted as is every author to his publishers from commissioning editor, assistant editor to the sub-editor and everyone in between. I thank them for their diligence and enthusiasm. In particular thank you to Caitlin Cornish, Aimee Dibbens, Jennie Kitchin, Samantha Hartley and Viv Wickham. And of course to our copy editor who made sense of everything and presented a polished professional final work of art . . . thank you Tessa Hanford. Drinks on us for you all.

I am of course also indebted to my tireless co-author and friend, Paresh Kiri. Paresh, like me, co-founded a hedge fund. The one for which he developed strategies went on to become a $2 billion fund. I am pleased to be able to thrash out our thoughts and ideas in this book and publish some of those 'recipes of trading success'. We know the cake rises when the ingredients are right, but also the oven, that is the environment, has to be right too.

About the Authors

ALPESH PATEL

Alpesh launched asset management company Praefinium Partners in 2004. He is a former Visiting Fellow in Business and Industry at Corpus Christi College, Oxford University. He has written 13 books on trading, translated into 8 languages. For Bloomberg TV he co-presented shows for three years as their in-house online trading specialist. He has had over 200 columns on trading published in the *Financial Times* through his 'Diary of an Internet Trader' column.

Alpesh won the competition in the *Financial Times* to predict the value of the FTSE 100 over a 12 month period coming within 0.5% of the final value. He is the founder of www.investingbetter.com which is an online trading education company and has his own investment software in partnership with Sharescope, called the 'Alpesh Patel Special Edition' of Sharescope.

Alpesh has lectured on trading from Beijing and San Francisco to Guatemala and from Spain to India, Singapore and Hong Kong.

Alpesh is also the founder of www.alpeshpatel.com offering trading education.

PARESH KIRI

Paresh Kiri has vast experience as a floor trader on the world's second largest derivatives exchange – LIFFE – and as a portfolio manager spanning some 18 years. He is an FSA regulated investment manager.

Starting his career on the LIFFE floor in 1993, Paresh was one of the first traders to embrace screen trading, through the LIFFE online trading platform APT (Automated Pit Trading). Making progress under the guidance of legendary LIFFE trader, David Kyte, he was one of the most consistent traders on the largest product on the floor – the Japanese government bond.

After successfully completing the Investment Management Certificate in 1996 he was one of the founders of Kyte Securities. So from trading financial futures and option products, Paresh had his first taste of trading stocks and shares. During the next three years he was instrumental in discovering bespoke strategies for trading equities globally.

In 2000, Kyte Securities became Eden Financial – which is now one of the most respected wealth management companies in the City of London – and the strategies developed were then incorporated as the backbone to the Tomahawk hedge fund, run by Marble Bar Asset Management. That fund went on to manage over $2 billion of assets.

Since leaving Eden Financial in 1999, Paresh has been managing private client and institutional money, and developing very specific operational services going back to Kyte Group to assist with the development of an Index Options Desk, and seeking ways of bringing the strategies he developed to the wider public audience by structuring managed accounts services using online trading platforms.

Paresh regularly coaches and holds private seminars on trading the markets. Paresh sits on the Advisory Board of Sterling Group (www.sterlinggroup.info) which has its HQ in Dubai.

Introduction

Wall Street's favorite scam is pretending luck is skill.

—Ron Ross

NEVER HAVE SO FEW MADE SO MUCH

In the middle of the last decade, money managers, i.e. professional traders, earned a fortune. Never in the history of economic endeavour has so much been earned by so few so quickly. They were led by Long Island fund manager James Simons of Renaissance Technologies who earned $1.5 billion, followed by T. Boone Pickens Jr of Texas with $1.4 billion, and New York investor George Soros with $840 million.

So what is the attitude of the professional trader? The ones who make the big sums. First and foremost, I want to get you investing – successfully. That means I am a pragmatist. I measure the success of this book by the money you make, not by the exams you pass.

Overriding all else, I believe in simplicity, saving time and making money. These are the core principles. If you like lots of equations and complexity and never investing or making money – then this book is not for you.

BUT SURELY YOU CAN'T TEACH THE COMPLEXITIES OF THE MARKETS IN ONE BOOK?

As an experienced trader I have met PhD graduates who make money and people who left school at 16 who make money. You can choose to make money using your academic brilliance, or by some other strategy. We want to get across the simpler strategies. The ones that are based on seeing the profitable wood and missing the trees, avoiding the noise and hearing the music or to carry the book's analogy forward – smelling the sweet aroma of the cooking and not being bogged down in the minutiae of how an oven works.

So you can try to work out how the US dollar/euro will move by studying Figure I.1 but you probably don't need to. We do know that the style used in Figure I.2, which shows the price chart of US dollar versus Norwegian krone, is going to save you a lot of time.

So, would you prefer to analyse the data shown in Figure I.1? (The answer is no.)
OR would you rather use Figure I.2? (The answer is yes.)
Or something as simple and clear as shown in Figure I.3?

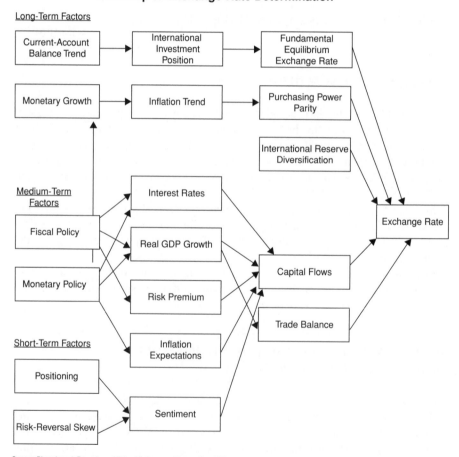

Roadmap to Exchange-Rate Determination

Source: *Bloomberg & Rosenberg, Michael R. Currency Forecasting*, 1996

Figure I.1   Roadmap to exchange rate determination
Source: Bloomberg and Rosen, Michael R., *Currency Forecasting*, 1996

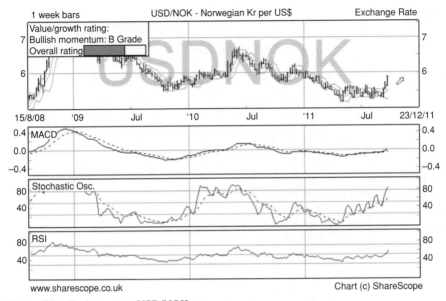

Figure I.2   Exchange rate USD/NOK

Source: www.sharescope.co.uk. © ShareScope, reproduced with permission

The following explains how an analysis is carried out:

- Find a trend, e.g. a downward trend (1)
- Locate a breakout from that trend to the upside, i.e. where the price moves higher (2) as a purchase point

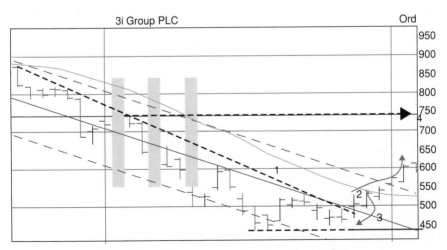

Figure I.3   A simple strategy based on price breakout

Table I.1   The day trader in Microsoft stock futures

08:00	At desk, make sure computer is up and running, data being collected
08:05	Go through latest headlines on financial websites to check what has happened overnight
08:20	Make a note of likely pivot points and supports and resistances for the day based on past week's action and yesterday's action
08:30	Monitor market but as per system do not enter before 10:00
10:00	View momentum indicators on 3-minute and 5-minute charts of likely buy or short signals
10:15	Possible buy signal. Ready to click on buy, wait. No, false alarm
10:30	Still no signal, continue watching
10:40	Possible signal to short. Confirmed. Click on sell and enter order
10:41	Five sold. Make note of stop-loss (and print out price chart)
10:42	While monitoring prices, draw on price chart possible target levels, supports and resistances
10:45	Price rises. Doubts creeping in
10:50	Price hits within points of stop-loss. Indicators still suggest holding position
11:00	Position still open
11:02	Price now running up quickly, indicators not showing sell, with paper profits eroded. Trailing stop near, get ready to close
11:05	Price continues dropping
11:15	Price starts rising. Momentum on 3-minute chart suggests exit
11:16	Momentum on 3- and 5-minute charts suggest exit, The MACD (moving average convergence divergence), an indicator of price momentum, still suggests in
11:17	Trailing stop hit. Exit
11:18	Hit sell order, wait for fill price: five bought and position closed
11:19	Reconfigure for next trade. Return to screen

- Set a stop-loss, i.e. know when you are wrong, e.g. price resumes a downward trend (3)
- Set a profit target based on a reasonable recent price level (4)
- Ensure reward target (Reward – Entry) is greater than risk (Entry – Stop-loss) ((4 – 2) > (2 – 3))

To give you an even better idea of how short-term active traders may spend their time, consider Table I.1 (of course you are not required to be a short-term trader, which is why we include strategies for every hue of trader).

HOW WE KNOW EXPERTS LET US DOWN

The only way to measure an expert's worth is by the performance of their stock ideas. If you could just as easily put money into an index tracker, which simply follows the

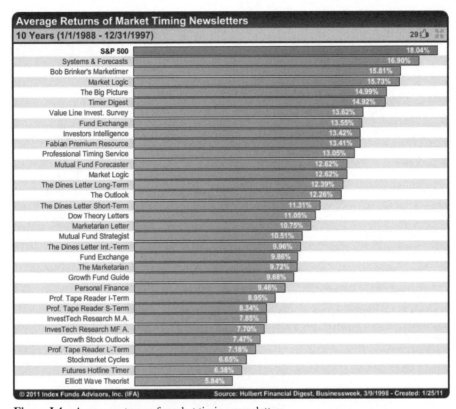

Figure I.4 Average returns of market timing newsletters
Source: Hulbert Financial Digest, Businessweek, 3 September 1998, created 25 January 2011. © Index
Funds Advisors, Inc

performance of the Dow or FTSE, then why waste time and money with an expert?
And we know experts don't always perform. Just look at Figure I.4.

We need to know that it is not all about the right recipe, but also the right mindset.

We would be doing our readers a disservice if we just gave you a load of strategies
and left you to it. That does not make for success. We know this because, as any
experienced trader will tell you, you need to be able to execute the strategy and not let
emotion and indiscipline get in the way. Figures I.5 and I.6 show a common trading
problem.

One final question: is it the right time to be even thinking about trading or investing?
And that is a fair question, between record budget deficits, sovereign debt defaults,
the largest bankruptcies in history and potential collapse of currencies, should we
just put our money under the mattress?

Well, most of our strategies do not depend on the markets moving in one direction.
That is why we think you are better off handling your own money than stashing

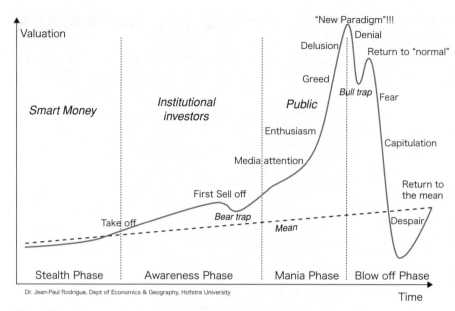

Figure I.5 Average returns of market timing newsletters
Source: Dr Jean-Paul Rodrigue, Department of Economics and Geography, Hofstra University, reproduced with permission

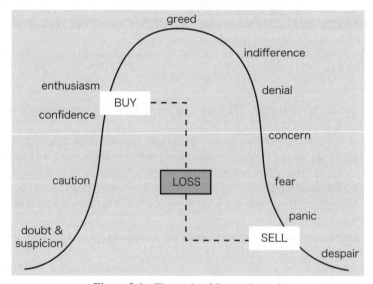

Figure I.6 The cycle of fear and greed

Market Turmoil and the Dow Jones Industrial Average 83 Years (1/1/1928 - 12/31/2010)					
Date	Event	DJIA Close Previous Day	DJIA Close	DJIA % Change	One Year Change
1 10/29/29	Black Tuesday	260.64	230.07	-11.73%	-17.10%
2 9/1/39	World War II Begins	134.41	135.25	0.62%	-4.07%
3 12/7/41	Japan Attacks Pearl Harbor	115.90	112.52	-2.92%	2.20%
4 6/25/50	North Korea Invades South Korea	224.35	213.91	-4.65%	14.67%
5 11/22/63	President Kennedy Assassinated	732.65	711.49	-2.89%	24.99%
6 1/31/65	Escalation of Vietnam War	902.86	903.68	0.09%	8.83%
7 8/9/74	President Nixon Resigns	784.89	777.30	-0.97%	5.98%
8 11/4/79	Iran Hostage Crisis Begins	818.94	812.63	-0.77%	17.29%
9 3/30/81	President Reagan Shot	994.78	992.16	-0.26%	-16.90%
10 10/19/87	Black Monday	2,246.73	1,738.74	-22.61%	95.93%
11 1/16/91	Operation Desert Storm Begins	2,490.59	2,508.91	0.74%	29.52%
12 4/19/95	Oklahoma City Bombing	4,179.13	4,207.49	0.68%	31.56%
13 9/11/01	Terrorist Attacks of 9/11	9,605.51	8,920.70	-7.13%	-3.81%
14 3/19/03	Operation Iraqi Freedom Begins	8,194.23	8,265.45	0.87%	23.24%
15 9/15/08	Lehman Declares Bankruptcy	11,421.99	10,917.51	-4.42%	-15.58%

© 2011 Index Funds Advisors, Inc. (IFA)   Source: Yahoo! Finance - Created: 10/28/11

Figure I.7　Market turmoil and the Dow Jones industrial average
Source: Yahoo! Finance, created 28 October 2011. © 2011 Index Funds Advisors, Inc

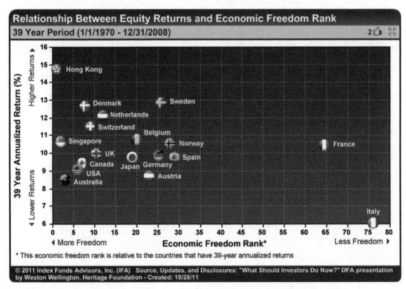

Figure I.8　Relationship between equity returns and economic freedom rank
Source: Updates and disclosures: 'What should investors do now?' DFA presentation by Weston Wellington, Heritage Foundation, created 28 October 2011. © 2011 Index Funds Advisors, Inc

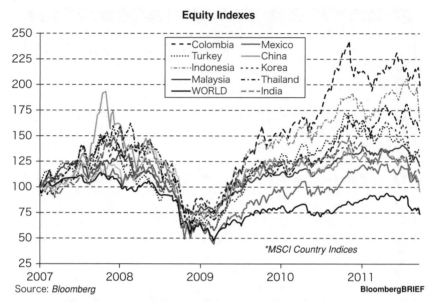

Figure I.9 Equity indexes
Source: Bloomberg

it in a safebox. If the markets fall, there are still strategies to profit from. Equally, let's get some perspective here. We hope that Figures I.7–I.9 show that even in the darkest moments the markets rebound, and as long as there is economic freedom, we survive.

Part I
APERITIF

The following strategies are suitable for the beginner trader and investor. They work, are easy to use and, for most people, are the only strategies they may ever need. For others, they comprise part of their armoury of strategies depending on the markets in which they are trading.

> The decline of the aperitif may well be one of the most depressing phenomena of our time.
>
> —Luis Buñuel (Spanish film director)

Recipe 1
Uncle's Favourite
Difficulty Level: Beginner

No one in his right mind would walk into the cockpit of an airplane and try to fly it, or into an operating theater and open a belly. And yet they think nothing of managing their retirement assets. I've done all three, and I'm here to tell you that managing money is, in its most critical elements (the quota of emotional discipline and quantitative ability required) even more demanding than the first two.

—William Bernstein

HISTORY OF THE RECIPE

Traders hate having to use their brains. They hate having to predict. They prefer to make things as automated as possible. Who wouldn't? So wouldn't it be helpful if, when we were trading, we could be pretty sure where a price will go? The essence of this trading strategy is that prices go back to where they were in the recent past.

This strategy is used by professionals and by novices and so should be simple enough for beginners to apply. The principle is 'mean reverting' – that is the price 90% of the time does not move in any trend but just back and forth.

Take a look at Figure 1.1. I have chosen the 3-minute chart, where each individual bar represents 3 minutes of price moves. I have taken this one from Sterling-markets.com, a broker that provides charting free as part of its brokerage services and one which I frequently use.

This strategy is used by professionals and by novices and so should be simple enough for beginners to apply. The principle is 'mean reverting' – that is the price 90% of the time does not move in any trend but just back and forth.

Figure 1.1   GBP/USD 3-minute chart
Source: © Sterlingmarkets.com, reproduced with permission

I have drawn a horizontal line pointing to 1.551, which I estimate to be the average or mean around which the price moves and to which it seems to revert. Some software will do this using a 'linear regression', which is a statistician's way of saying 'the average price over a period of time'. But I find it is accurate enough to do it by eye and in a fast-trading environment saves time anyway.

I could have looked at different time frames and then of course the mean would have been different and so would our trades. So who uses the 3-minute chart? Well, certainly someone who is trading actively during the day. They may even trade on the 1-minute chart. They do this because it gives them lots of trades and allows them to deploy their capital and get a return on it.

Figure 1.2 illustrates the daily chart, where each bar represents one whole day of price moves in GBP/USD. The average or mean I have drawn comes to around 1.58. Again the idea is that the price, even if it extends far away from this number, either above or below, tends to move back to this mean value.

Does the price actually revert to the mean? Very often yes. But given that we could lose lots of money if it didn't, we must as part of this strategy put in stop-losses to protect our capital.

Why did this strategy develop? Because usually traders do not like predicting trends. They want to have a better idea of where the price is heading based on where it has been, not where it might go based on where it has never been.

Below are three more illustrations. Figure 1.3 is another example of mean reverting. Figure 1.4 shows an example where a currency does not revert to mean and Figure 1.5 depicts the essential concept of 'mean reversion', that is there is an area of value around which a price will oscillate. Therefore our risk of the price not reverting to the mean is reduced because even if a new area of value is picked by the markets it

Figure 1.2 GBP/USD daily chart
Source: © Sterlingmarkets.com, reproduced with permission

Figure 1.3 GBP/USD daily chart showing 1.62 as an area around which the price seems to be mean reverting

Figure 1.4 GBP/USD showing no mean reversion on the daily chart from November 2009 to June 2010. If we had expected the price to return to 1.7 USD per GBP we would have waited a long time and potentially suffered a large loss

happens infrequently. And if the price does move sharply against us to this new area, our stop-loss exit will prevent too large a loss on those occasions.

INGREDIENTS

- The rules
- Web charting

RECIPE

1. **Choose your time frame.** Do you trade all day, sitting in front of a computer? In this case choose a 3-minute or 5-minute chart. Or are you busy most of the day

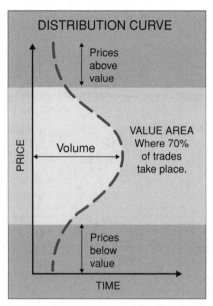

Figure 1.5 A graphical depiction of the principle of mean reversion. That is the price tends to move around a central 'value area' or mean

doing other things and so cannot be monitoring the markets every minute? Here a daily chart may be better, where each bar is the move of a whole day's worth of price changes.

2. **Choose a mean reversion line.** You will need a sufficient time frame of history on which to base the fact there is a mean around which the price oscillates. Only then can we choose a mean reversion line. In Figure 1.6 we have marked where we think the mean is by the horizontal line. Notice there are over 100 historical bars covered by this line. This tells me that the price has been moving around this mean for quite a while and the assumption I then make is it will continue to do so. This can be done by 'eye' as an estimate when looking at the chart, which is how I do it. Or it can be done on financial planning websites that provide charts by using the 'linear regression' line between a historic point and today's price.

3. **Choose an entry point** at which to trigger your trade. For instance Point A in Figure 1.6 represents when we felt the price had moved too far from the mean and will begin to revert back to it. How do we pick this point? We could use complicated statistical measures such as standard deviations. But let's keep it simple. For me the entry is 1.5500. This is because:

   a. it looks like a level which the price tends not to reach too frequently
   b. it is far from the mean and so is likely to result in a good catch
   c. it is not so far from the mean that it is the start of a whole new trend

Entry: 1.5500. Mean reversion line: 1.5525.

Figure 1.6 GBP/USD 3-minute chart. Mean reversion line = 1.5525. Point A (entry) = 1.5500. Point B (worst price) = 1.5485. Point C (exit) = 1.5525
Source: © Sterlingmarkets.com, reproduced with permission

So how much would I make? Well, if I made $1 for every point from entry to exit at the mean reversion line, then I would make $25. (Of course you can trade multiples of that, depending on how much trading capital you have, but more on that in a moment.) 1.5525 – 1.5500 = 25.

This exit actually only happened at point C. It took a bit longer than expected, but got there in the end. But doesn't that mean you are hanging around for a long time with a lot of capital tied up? Not so, as on multiple currencies and commodities you can place multiple positions. This diversifies your risk (assuming they are not all the same time frame of 3 minutes and all USD trades – but even then you would get some diversification, i.e. they would not all be moving in tandem and so are not the same bet over and over again until it becomes one large single bet which could go wrong and expose you to large risk).

Point B represented our worst moment when the price went as low as 1.5485. At that point we were sitting on a paper loss of 1.5500 – 1.5485 = $15. How did we know not to exit at that point? Or put another way, what is our stop-loss, the point at which we exit with a loss? We cannot after all hold on forever in the hope of making $25.

If the stop-loss is equal to the profit to be achieved, i.e. $25 then that is a good measure. But surely then we win at $25 and we lose at $25, so if the number of wins and losing trades is the same, we don't make any money. This is true, actually after brokerage costs we would be losing a little.

But this is where the principle of mean reversion comes in. If we expect prices that have fallen quite far to rebound like on a bungee or a string of spaghetti, then we expect to win more often (i.e. prices extended from the mean, revert back to it) than lose (prices go on extending and make ever greater losses for us and do not mean revert). So imagine we were therefore expecting to be right, i.e. the price reverts back to the mean, 6 times out of 10, and wrong a whopping 4 times out of 10.

Then our results would look like this:

$$\text{Profits} = 6 \times \$25 = \$150$$
$$\text{Losses} = 4 \times \$25 = \$100$$
$$\text{Overall profits per 10 trades} = \$50$$

More heat: But hang on. If we've found a profit-making machine, why don't we just make bigger bets, like 10 times the size? After all, we will make 10 times the profits. The reply is: what if we have a string of losses? Imagine we used 100 times larger sizes. And we had five losing trades. We would be down $5 \times \$2,500$, that is $10,000. If your trading capital was $10,000 then you would be wiped out.

More sauce: Okay, but suppose your trading capital is not merely $10,000. How do you then decide how much to bet in each trade to maximise your return? After all you don't want to make a pathetic $25 now that you've discovered a profit-making strategy. As mentioned in the introduction to this book, when you are wrong, than ideally you should lose no more 2% of your trading capital. If you have $12,500, then that would mean you lose no more than $250 when you are wrong on any one trade.

That would mean you would have $6 \times \$250$ winning trades, making you $1,500 and $4 \times \$250$ losing trades, losing you $1,000. Overall for every 10 trades you make $500 profit.

Entry

- Draw a mean reversion line.
- Go long as price falls (or vice versa)
- Start with small $1 per point move profit or loss, for example if the GBP/USD rate moves 0.0001 you should make $1. Build trade size so that any exit at a loss is 2% of total trading capital

Exit

- If price hits mean reversion line or stop-loss

But what could go wrong with such a delicious recipe that has you salivating on its description? See the next section on money management and risk.

VARIATIONS TO THE RECIPE

Money and Risk Management

Be careful not to experiment too much. When does this strategy turn sour? When your discipline leaks like a sieve. Namely when you do not exit with discipline at your stop-loss because you don't want to take the loss. Or you get greedy and do not exit at the mean reversion line. Or you make the trade size so large, that a couple of bad trades and your capital is all eaten up in losses.

Why not enter at closer to the mean reversion line? After all the price will revert. It is true you could. And your stop-loss should be proportionately set. But you will potentially make less money, because the move is small from a closer entry point.

Okay, you ask, **why not increase the bet size and trade from a closer distance?** Nothing wrong with that. As long as you stick to your stop-loss. The problem is the price could just keep hitting your stop-loss, i.e. continue away from the mean reversion line. The point of us picking Point A is that it is unlikely to go on beyond that value based on recent price action seen from the price chart. So your next question is . . .

Why not enter close to the mean reversion line, and put the stop-loss a lot further out? The answer is that you could as long as [number of winning trades] × [$ profit per winning trade] is greater than [number of losing trades] × [$ loss per losing trade].

So imagine you entered when the price moved $10 away from the mean reversion line. And your stop-loss was $100 loss away. That is if you suffered a $100 loss you would exit. This is fine as long as you had 10 winning trades for every losing one.

So take the example shown in Figure 1.7. You place a stop-loss very far away. You then just keep entering trades as you see fit as soon as they move from the mean reversion line. What could go wrong?

Well, as mentioned above:

- You have a string of losses and wipe out your account. For instance let us say you had all these positions open and your stop-loss was hit.

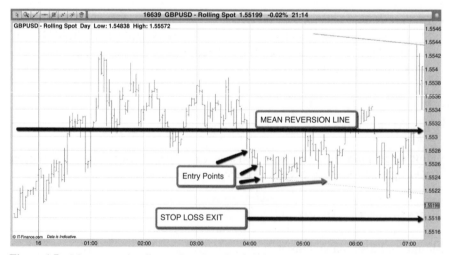

Figure 1.7   Mean reversion line and entry and exit points
Source: © Sterlingmarkets.com, reproduced with permission

We avoid that by following the above rules of limiting our bet size and making sure if we have a string of, say, five consecutive losing trades, we do not come even close to wiping ourselves out. In fact five consecutive losing trades should lose no more than a total of 10% of our total trading capital.

HERE'S ONE I MADE EARLIER

Figure 1.8 illustrates the results from this strategy using actual trading results. The chart shows 454 trades placed in the first two weeks of July – 450 trades won. Each horizontal line shows the level of profit per trade. Why was it not exactly the same profit per trade? Because the strategy represents all trades, across all time frames and products.

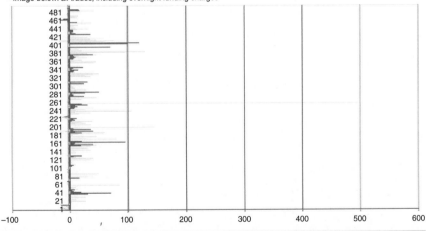

Individual Closed Trades Returns 1st–17th July 2009

The Managed Account Commenced in June 2009 on five accounts. All accounts show returns between +30% and +100% on capital deposited

• Total trades:454 trades (excl funding overnight funding charges)

• Winning trades: 450

• Losing trades: 4

• Average return: £14.79 (after all overnight funding charges costs)

• Maximum: £500. Minimum: £-35

• Total overnight funding charges: £406.75

• Image below: all trades, including overnight funding charges

Figure 1.8   All trades and the profit or loss corresponding to that trade

Recipe 2
What Good Dishes Taste Like –
The Recipe for Trading Success
Difficulty Level: Beginner

Nobody told me there'd be days like these.

—John Lennon

Do you dream of becoming a professional hedge fund manager? Want to know what a professional hedge fund manager's monthly returns look like? Trading strategies are all different but the outcome should be the same in terms not just of returns but also of how those returns are distributed. For instance you would not call it much of a recipe if it gave you a positive return but took until 300 losing trades and 1 winning trade to do so.

Bill Lipschutz used to be Global Head of Forex Trading at Salomon Brothers. He set up Hathersage Capital Management. His performance figures are typical of a quality fund manager – regardless of trading strategy. I first met Bill in 1996 when I interviewed him for my first book, *The Mind of a Trader.*

Figure 2.1 shows in how many months he produces any given return. So, for instance, 36 months have resulted in a 0–1% monthly return. About 4 months have resulted in a −3 to −4% monthly return.

Why will your trading results eventually look like this if you are successful over a long period of time in applying the strategies in this book? Well let's break it down.

You cannot be right 100% of the time. So out of 10 trades you will probably look to be right 6 or 7 times. After all 5 times out of 10 is the same as a coin toss. But of course it is not about how often you are right, but how much money you make when you are right. So whilst you could make money being right only 4 times out of 10, most people want to be comfortable and right more often than wrong.

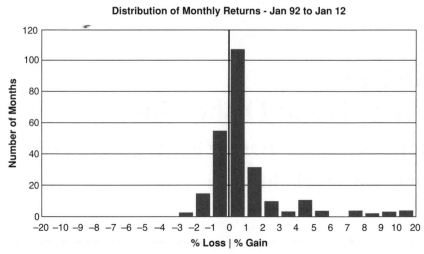

Figure 2.1   Distribution of monthly returns by Hathersage's Long Term Currency Programme
Source: Hathersage, Bloomberg LP, reproduced with permission

Equally, when you win and are right, you cannot expect to have huge wins. It would be nice, but most winning trades are small gains. So how does that translate into your trading outcome? It means you have many months of small gains. And a few months of big wins. You also have losing months. But fewer of these (because there will be 3 or 4 losing trades out of 10). So the most critical factor left is to ensure when you do lose you do not lose big; that the 3 or 4 losing trades do not wipe out your gains.

> Equally, when you win and are right, you cannot expect to have huge wins. It would be nice, but most winning trades are small gains.

Guess what most private investors get wrong? They have few wins and their losing trades wipe them out. So in this book we focus very much on ensuring that you have few losing trades and the losses, when they necessarily happen, are kept small.

Bill Lipschutz's performance figures in Figure 2.2 show that any decent trading system has to be able to bet small enough to survive several moving months and indeed losing years. This can only be done when one is risking say 1–2% of total capital on any one trade. Again, this is not something that is obvious to most private investors. But if you work on the basis that you will have as many losing months as one of the world's leading traders, then you suddenly realise it must be the case.

After all, Bill had two consecutive losing years (2005 and 2006). And in 2006–7 he had seven consecutive losing months. You can only survive seven consecutive losing

(returns are net of all fees)

	Jan	Feb	Mar	Apr	May	Jun	Jul	Aug	Sep	Oct	Nov	Dec	YTD
2011	0.10	(0.59)	2.01	0.49	(0.50)	(1.47)	(0.88)	0.85	0.54	(1.42)	0.34	(0.10)	(0.68%)
2010	(0.74)	0.89	0.24	0.58	4.11	0.94	(0.05)	1.25	1.44	0.25	0.88	(0.15)	9.97%
2009	1.10	0.29	0.60	3.11	(0.94)	0.34	0.13	0.47	0.28	0.23	0.13	0.31	6.15%
2008	0.78	1.46	1.25	1.41	(0.12)	(0.84)	0.24	0.45	2.37	0.83	1.13	2.86	12.42%
2007	(0.28)	(0.34)	0.06	(0.74)	(0.15)	(0.11)	0.15	(0.60)	0.64	0.47	2.43	0.16	1.67%
2006	(0.04)	(0.10)	0.17	(0.20)	0.25	(0.43)	0.01	(1.21)	(0.85)	(0.25)	(0.35)	(0.30)	(2.93%)
2005	0.30	(1.47)	0.36	1.02	0.45	0.49	(0.76)	0.18	(1.19)	0.41	(0.25)	(0.90)	(2.55%)
2004	(0.50)	0.61	0.18	0.21	0.24	(0.71)	0.65	0.55	(1.11)	(0.09)	1.05	1.48	3.39%
2003	1.08	0.03	(0.02)	(0.67)	0.84	5.66	1.66	0.12	1.26	(0.20)	(0.43)	0.03	10.58%
2002	0.69	0.35	(0.63)	0.29	(1.17)	0.24	(0.04)	1.01	1.69	(0.35)	0.42	(0.43)	1.08%
2001	0.79	0.06	2.93	0.23	(1.89)	0.04	(1.30)	(0.31)	0.77	0.63	(1.49)	3.71	4.16%
2000	(0.42)	0.06	0.89	1.76	(0.09)	(1.26)	(0.47)	0.14	(0.53)	0.90	2.13	(0.47)	1.07%
1999	0.35	16.48	0.44	0.47	7.20	0.00	(0.38)	0.42	(0.21)	(0.14)	(1.18)	(0.75)	15.68%
1998	0.06	0.16	0.38	0.03	(1.08)	8.32	9.34	0.42	16.05	4.30	0.35	4.41	63.43%
1997	4.48	5.22	10.84	0.07	0.10	0.00	0.05	0.04	0.06	0.03	0.02	(0.03)	20.78%
1996	1.01	4.34	2.86	(1.11)	1.30	1.61	0.07	0.09	0.04	2.68	0.02	1.91	15.70%
1995	0.26	0.07	0.43	0.15	0.86	(2.02)	0.21	0.02	0.04	0.08	4.37	5.75	9.53%
1994	1.93	0.60	0.43	0.86	0.14	0.14	0.00	0.04	0.67	0.34	(0.81)	0.19	4.61%
1993	1.32	2.70	(0.26)	7.65	1.73	1.21	(0.78)	1.57	1.32	0.85	0.20	1.01	19.89%
1992	9.99	4.14	7.23	4.46	4.65	4.87	0.31	0.82	1.83	1.09	1.90	1.54	51.67%

Figure 2.2 Performance summary for Hathersage

months if you don't lose a lot. Obviously. And you can only restrict how much you lose if the total money lost in each losing trade is limited. Since we do not know if a trade will be winning or losing, then we can limit the amount of money we lose when we do have a losing trade by ensuring the total amount of money we put in any one trade is a small proportion of our total money.

But wait, doesn't that mean we are using very little of our capital? Isn't that a waste of our resources? Not if we are placing lots of different uncorrelated trades. How? By trading over different time frames in different products such as commodities and stocks. But surely the same strategy doesn't work on all of these? No, hence this book has many strategies.

You can only restrict how much you lose if the total money lost in each losing trade is limited. Since we do not know if a trade will be winning or losing, then we can limit the amount of money we lose when we do have a losing trade by ensuring the total amount of money we put in any one trade is a small proportion of our total money.

IT'S NOT JUST ABOUT THE RIGHT STRATEGY

Probably the single most important aspect of trading success is money management. Why? Imagine you have $100,000 to cook with. Now imagine you have a trading system where you are correct 60% of the time – i.e. a little better than a toss of a coin. Imagine that when you are correct, you double your money and when you are wrong you lose your money. How much of your $100,000 would you bet on each trade?

Well let's say you bet $10,000 on each trade. Let's also say you happened to lose four times in a row. It can happen. You would be down $40,000 or 40%. With $60,000 you need a greater than 50% return to break even.

Notice that. You lost 40%, but need to make more than 50% to break even. In other words, the more you lose the much more you need to break even. If you only lost 10% you would only need 11.1% to break even.

So any trading system money management rules have to ensure you do not lose too much from a series of losing trades. One way to do so is to ensure that on each position you can never lose more than a certain small percentage of your overall trading capital. For a professional trader that would mean never losing more than 1–2% ($1,000–$2,000 in the above example) of your trading capital.

Notice that. You lost 40%, but need to make more than 50% to break even. In other words, the more you lose the much more you need to break even. If you only lost 10% you would only need 11.1% to break even.

Table 2.1 How small losses mean big recoveries to recoup those losses

Drawdown	Gain to recover
5%	5.3%
10%	11.1%
15%	17.6%
20%	25%
25%	33%
30%	42.9%
40%	66.7%
50%	100%

It may seem ridiculously small, but the oven soon catches fire when you over-egg the pudding and bet the whole ranch on a few trades. Avoid the hangover – trade small sizes. It will get you big results.

Table 2.1 shows how a small loss, 'drawdown', results in a trader needing much larger gains with the pot of money left in order to recoup the money. Indeed, the gains needed are disproportionately greater than the losses incurred; so a 50% drop needs a 100% recovery of the money left.

OVER-EGGING THE PUDDING: HOW MUCH SHOULD I PLACE ON ANY ONE TRADE?

It is the knowledge of how to calculate the answer to this question that makes the main bedrock of a successful trading record. So should I have buried it in one part of one chapter of the book or should I have emblazoned it in the title of the whole book?

The problem with calling the book 'how much should I place on any one trade?' is the same problem the financial media face: how can we attract audiences? The difference with me is, I will give you your medicine – they too often only give you the sweet sugary title, the fluff.

If you risk too little on each trade, the returns will be too low to overcome transaction costs, small losses and overhead (quote feeds, electricity, rent, costs of books such as this, and so on).

Risk more and the returns will increase, but one bad trade and you are wiped out and have to explain to the spouse how you have had to cancel the annual vacation and pawn the mother-in-law.

Traders use different formulae to work out how much money they should put on any trade. Gibbons Burke in an outstanding article in the excellent *Active Trader* magazine provides one such useful formula.

> Risk more and the returns will increase, but one bad trade and you are wiped out and have to explain to the spouse how you have had to cancel the annual vacation and pawn the mother-in-law.

You can use this formula to determine how many shares of stock to buy (actually, the formula should have been the title of the book, but the publishers for some reason thought it might not make the *New York Times* Bestseller list if I did that):

$$x = \frac{p - er}{s}$$

where
  $s =$ size of the trade
  $e =$ portfolio equity (cash and holdings)
  $r =$ maximum risk percentage per trade
  $p =$ entry price on the trade
  $x =$ pre-determined stop-loss or exit price

Gibbons Burke gives the following example: 'Belinda has a trading account with a total value (cash and holdings) of $100,000 and is willing to risk 2% of that capital on any one trade. Her trading system gives her a signal to buy DTCM stock trading at $100 per share and the system says that the reversal point on that trade is $95. Plugging this into the formula tells Belinda that she can buy 400 shares of DTCM. The cost of this investment is $40,000, but she is only risking 2% of her capital, or $2,000, on the idea'.

Belinda then gets a tip from her brother-in-law that KRMA is about to take a nose dive from its lofty perch at $40 because he heard from his barber that earnings of KRMA will be well below expectations. She's willing to go short. She studies a KRMA chart and can't see any logical technical points that would be a good place to put in a stop, so she uses the money management method to determine the stop according to the above formula – rearranging it for x the stop-loss.

$$x = \frac{p - er}{s}$$

$p = \$40$; $e = \$100$ k; $r = 2\%$; $s = -400$ ('$-$' because you are shorting) $= 40 - (100 \text{ k} \times 2)/-400 = \$45$ stop-loss.

Placing these figures into the formula tells Belinda that her stop price on the short sale of KRMA should be $45. If she didn't want to assign a high confidence on this trade she could reduce the maximum risk to 1% ($r = 0.01$), which would bring the stop down to $42.5.

IT'S NOT ABOUT THE STOCKS YOU PICK

'10 stocks you must own now'; 'Companies that grow in good times and bad'. These are just some of the investment magazines' headlines you will have read.

On financial TV we know we have to bring you stock pickers, fund managers and analysts with stock ideas – otherwise you will not watch and even more importantly advertisers will not advertise. In financial TV we have even started using the techniques of tacky mainstream entertainment shows. For instance have you heard the financial TV presenters say, 'after the break we will tell you Alpesh's top three picks for the year ahead . . . don't go away, we'll be right back'?

There is only one thing wrong about all this. Market success has next to nothing to do with the stocks you pick. It has everything to do with money management – how much you stand to lose, when you increase your winning positions and exit your losing ones. Research proves it, and professional traders confirm it. Yet our obsession with stock picks continues. So, what are the most important investment questions you need answered?

'How much money should I put in any one trade?' Professional traders will tell you success is about 'the 2 × 2 rule'. Ensure your upside is twice your downside and never lose more than 2% of your trading capital in a single trade.

For instance with $20,000 capital, if you think Microsoft will go from $100 to $130 (30% gain), then you should equally not expect the stock to fall beyond $85 (15% loss). And that worst loss should total no more than 2% of your $20,000 capital, which is $400. So, you should only buy $2,670 of stock at $100 ($400 is 15% of $2,670).

'How much money should I put in any one trade?' Professional traders will tell you success is about 'the 2 × 2 rule'. Ensure your upside is twice your downside and never lose more than 2% of your trading capital in a single trade.

The formula (yes there is one, you don't think professionals trade by the seat of their pants do you?) is:

$$t = \frac{pr}{(e - x)}$$

where
    t = size of the trade
    p = portfolio size (cash and holdings)
    r = maximum risk percentage per trade
    e = entry price
    x = pre-determined stop-loss exit price

But surely if you are a good stock picker you don't need to worry about money management. Not true. If you gain 30% through stock picking, it only takes a 23% loss to bring you back to where you started. But if you lose 30%, it takes a much greater 43% through stock picking to just break even.

The same percentage loss and gain have unequal impact on your portfolio. Losses hurt more than gains benefit. The same percentage gain in the next trade from stock picking will not bail you out.

> If you gain 30% through stock picking, it only takes a 23% loss to bring you back to where you started. But if you lose 30%, it takes a much greater 43% through stock picking to just break even.

Why only 2%? Any more and you get too close to precipitous irrevocable losses from just a few trades. Let's say you have four consecutive losing trades, which is feasible for even the best stock pickers: a read of George Soros's trading diary in his *The Alchemy of Finance* confirms that.

And say you lose 5% of your portfolio on each trade. With the remainder of your portfolio you now need to make a gain greater than the world's second richest man and investor, Warren Buffett, achieves on average each year (23%). That's why it's not about the stocks you pick – whichever ones you pick, with poor money management you will suffer.

> 'Money management is like sex: Everyone does it, but not many like to talk about it and some do it better than others'.

Imagine two traders. Both make identical trades with their portfolio of $20,000. One bets $2,000 per trade and the other $10,000. Their results after four trades are +20%, −25%, −25%, +5% and −5%. A typical set of trades.

After just four trades, the second trader has underperformed the first by 22%. It was not the stocks they picked, after all both picked the same ones. It was down to money management.

If money management is so important then why are there not more internet sites devoted to it? Expert investor Gibbons Burke puts it best, 'Money management is like sex: Everyone does it, but not many like to talk about it and some do it better than others. But whilst sex sites on the web proliferate, sites devoted to the art and science of money management are somewhat difficult to find'. Put another way, you don't think a CEO of an online brokerage is a trader do you?

Still looking for a hot stock tip? Then I leave you with legendary investment academic William Bernstein who put it most honestly,

A decade ago, I really did believe that the average investor could do it himself. After all, the flesh was willing, the vehicles were available, and the math wasn't that hard. I was wrong. Having emailed and spoken to thousands of investors over the years, I've come to the sad conclusion that only a tiny minority, at most one percent, are capable of pulling it off. Heck, if the nation's largest pension funds can't get it right, what chance does John Q investor have? ('The Probability of Success', www.efficientfrontier.com/ef/103/probable.htm)

Me? I believe I'm in the top 1%. After all, George Soros is, why not me? How about you?

SUMMARY

- Losing small when inevitable losses come is best achieved by trading small relative to your overall capital, even if your trading system is right a majority of the time.

Recipe 3
Trend Lines and Channelling: Mind the Bumps
Difficulty Level: Beginner

The genius of investing is recognising the direction of a trend – not catching highs and lows.

—Unknown

Maybe the trend is your friend for a few minutes in Chicago, but for the most part it is rarely a way to get rich.

—Jim Rogers

HISTORY OF THE RECIPE

Keep things simple. Trend lines were created as a function of drawing a line between two points, and extending the line into the future. This is a much forgotten strategy and, if executed with due consideration for each new point, can yield dividends.

INGREDIENTS

All you need is web charting or charting software which displays basic line extension and provides the ability to join two points on a chart.

RECIPE

On 18 January 2011 MEDNAX Inc hit a new high for the year at $70.17. The very strong uptrend from September 2010 seems to be faltering but how do we really

Figure 3.1 MEDNAX chart: trend and entry points
Source: www.sharescope.co.uk. © ShareScope, reproduced with permission

know if it has ended; or if it will continue? It is important to create a strategy that will enable us to make more than we risk. Are we looking to go long, short or do nothing? The chart shown in Figure 3.1 allows us to consider all three.

Let us start by using our trend utensil. Using the **Trend Line**, we can draw a line by joining points **A** and **B**.

The first thing to do is to draw the trend line, using the dips, and then copy that line against the peaks finding in both cases the line of best fit. It will very rarely be exact but as you can see a channel can be found. So we can already draw some conclusions from this very basic study:

- The price has broken out of the channel and we now have to exercise some discipline. We could have gone short on the first breakout, but it may have been a false breakout, so perhaps we need to sit on our hands and see if the price will resume its journey and attempt to recover the trend.
- We could have had a sell order in just below the line at $67.80.

Cooking Tip: Do not undercook the dish. Be as certain as you can be.

So we then look a bit further back in time and discover a missing ingredient! Figure 3.2 shows that in 2008 MEDNAX Inc was trading at this same high. This

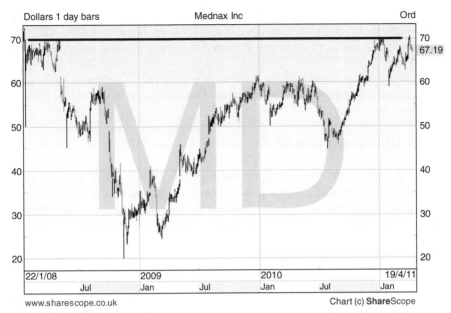

Figure 3.2   MEDNAX share price showing the horizontal resistance bar around $70
Source: www.sharescope.co.uk. © ShareScope, reproduced with permission

should encourage us to tuck in on the first break! The high is considered to be **long-term resistance** (i.e. a point the price hits but finds difficulty moving beyond) and so a first break of the trend line near this high should be a good trade.

VARIATIONS TO THE RECIPE

From this it must be noted that trend lines do exist. Support and resistance lines also exist. The two together, when applied over longer time frames, are the most positive combination. Over shorter time frames, it is harder to be as certain, as they have not been tested. The more often a price is tested and not breached, the more solid must be the resistance.

MORE ON THE RECIPE

The first thing to assess is the basic support, resistance and any strong trend. The stronger the trend or support line, then the greater the move away from it on a significant break. To decide if it is significant enough we need to calculate the **average true range (ATR)**.

The ATR is just a very simple measure of **volatility** and was developed by J. Welles Wilder. It helps us monitor any increase in activity from the average daily ATR that may result in a change of direction. You need to be sure the daily range is at least 2 × ATR.

The best place is to have a stop at the position that proves we are wrong. This could be just above $70.50, i.e. above the resistance line.

HERE'S ONE I MADE EARLIER

On 29 December 2009 Microsoft hit a new high for the year at 3,149.50 US cents. The very strong uptrend from March 2009 seems to be faltering but how do we know if it has ended, or if it will continue? Figure 3.3 shows us the trend line. Are we looking to go long, short or do nothing? Figure 3.3 allows us to consider all three.

Figure 3.3   Microsoft daily rolling price
Source: © Sterlingmarkets.com, reproduced with permission

On 12 January 2010 Microsoft tested just below 3,000 US cents. This was a key resistance on the way up and should have been good support on the way down. All we had to do was to place a sell order at or around 2,950 US cents and wait.

For Microsoft the ATR for the past 12 months on the daily chart = 55 cents by our calculation (Figure 3.4). Armed with this information we know that anything greater than 2 × ATR is an unusual move, i.e. $1.10 USD move. On Friday 22 January, Microsoft had a range (i.e. the price difference between the highest and lowest price the stock traded that day) of $1.96. Something has changed on this day for Microsoft. We do not know what but we will wait for confirmation that the trend may have changed. On this day the move was 3.5 × ATR.

Opened: 3000, High: 3020, Low: 2824, Close: 2896.

Figure 3.4   Microsoft daily rolling price
Source: © Sterlingmarkets.com, reproduced with permission

What Next!

Now we have established that there is an opportunity to go **short** Microsoft. Do we just sell or is there anything else we need to know? Well yes – it would be nice to know

- where to get out if we are WRONG (STOP)
- where to get out if we are RIGHT (LIMIT)
- if we have an appropriate risk/reward ratio, i.e. we want to make more than we are risking!
- how much money do we have at risk

Where to Place the stop

The best place is to have a stop at the position that proves we are wrong to be short for this short-term move. This could be just above the 3,000 US cents resistance line. To give it room we can say 3,030 US cents. So our entry was a point below 3,000.

On Friday 22 January our sell order would have been executed and with a stop at 3,030, our risk is 80 US cents per share.

Recipe 4
Japanese as Easy as Sushi: Exotic but not Complicated
Difficulty Level: Beginner

The Japanese have a great saying: 'When the student is ready, the Buddha will appear'.

—Mort Meyerson

HISTORY OF THE RECIPE

This strategy involves candlestick charting techniques, thought to have been developed in Japan over 400 years ago. But that does not make it complicated even if it is exotic. Japanese rice farmers would plot the movements of rice prices. They discovered that certain price patterns occurred before certain price moves. They therefore reasoned that if they could find such patterns then they could forecast the subsequent price moves.

Candlestick chart: The chart contains opening, high, low and closing values of a security for a time period. The hollow or filled part of the chart is known as the 'real body'. The long thin lines above and below the body indicate the high/low range and are called 'shadows' (also referred to as 'wicks' and 'tails'). The high range is marked at the top of the upper shadow, while the low range is marked at the bottom of the lower shadow. If a stock's closing price is higher than its opening price, then a hollow candlestick is drawn, the bottom of the body indicates the opening price and the top indicates the closing price. On the other hand, if a stock's closing price is lower than its opening price, a filled candlestick is drawn, where the top indicates the opening price and the bottom the closing price. See Figures 4.1 and 4.2.

Candlestick Formation

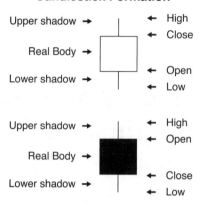

Figure 4.1   Candlestick formation

A candlestick chart is a slightly more sophisticated visual representation of the bar chart. It helps an investor or trader to develop trading strategies in order to maximise profit potential. It also demonstrates investor sentiment during a particular period of time.

All the price patterns have some psychological explanation behind them. Some examples are shown in Table 4.1.

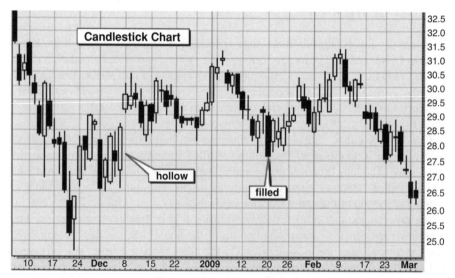

Figure 4.2   Candlestick chart

Table 4.1 Psychological explanations of price patterns

Pattern	Psychology	How often accurate in my experience
Bearish Shooting Star	The prices are driven higher and close higher for three consecutive days. On the final day, they do indeed move higher, they even close higher than the previous day, but the sellers drive them to close near the lower end of the range for that particular day. This suggests that buying pressure has lost momentum and a change in direction is imminent	55%
Bearish Evening Doji Star	The price-rise momentum shows some weakness when the open and closing prices are the same, even though the price gapped (i.e. did not trade certain prices but jumped from one price straight to a different level) higher from the previous day And then the next day the price opens lower and closes lower suggesting the bullish run is over and prices will continue to fall	70%
Bearish Engulfing Pattern	The final day opens higher than the previous day and closes below it. This suggests that traders tried to continue the momentum of the previous few days, by opening higher, but were unable to get the buy orders and indeed the market was so weak it even traded below the previous day's lowest price point	65%
Bullish Inverted Hammer	After days of selling, the bears start to worry the falls may be coming to an end as the price tries to rise and closes up slightly compared to the previous period. The long shadow on the final day is critical. It is buyers testing the waters and this spooks bears and often marks the reversal in a downward trend	55%
Bullish Harami	A small trading range with the price closing higher than when it opened the period suggests that bulls have found a floor and can fight off the selling by the bears. The buyers are able to resist falling prices	55%

INGREDIENTS

All you need is web charting or charting software which displays Japanese candle-sticks. And today most do, if they show price charts at all.

RECIPE

One of my favourites is the Bullish Island Reversal (aka Bullish Morning Doji Star). The reason is that not all Japanese price patterns are created equal. Some of the less frequent ones like this tend to be the most accurate. In my experience it is right 70% of the time.

Look for the set up shown in Figure 4.3.

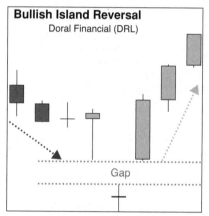

Figure 4.3   Bullish Island Reversal
Source: Tradecision (www.tradecision.com). © 2008 Investopedia.com

Notice how the price has been falling. Then there is a gap where the price opens and closes at the same level (doji star), before reversing the trend and starting to rise during the next day. Essentially what has happened is that the sellers have run out of steam, and the price gap exhausts their last selling efforts. So once they have exhausted their selling resources, and overdone the selling, the buyers come in without much resistance.

If there is no gap before or after, then this is not a valid signal.

VARIATIONS TO THE RECIPE

Of course the opposite holds true too. See Figure 4.4.

Even if not an exact carbon copy, I will look for close patterns, such as shown in Figure 4.5.

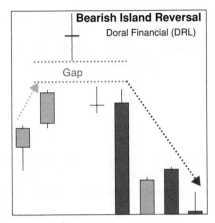

Figure 4.4   Bearish Island Reversal
Source: Tradecision (www.tradecision.com). © 2008 Investopedia.com

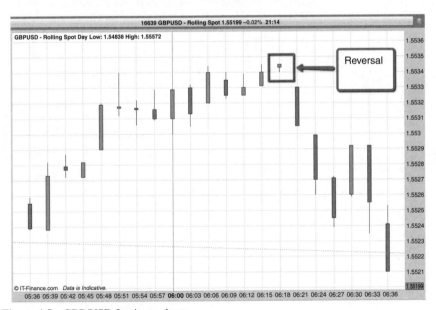

Figure 4.5   GBP/USD 3-minute charts
Source: © www.sterlingmarkets.com, reproduced with permission

MORE ON THE RECIPE

Of course this only tells you the likelihood of reversal. Your stop-loss needs to be set – I suggest the start of the gap is a good place (i.e. in the case of a bearish reversal – the lower price at which the gap commences). Your profit target has to be greater than the loss you could suffer if you were to be stopped out. And this is important because your likely reward has to be greater than your likely loss.

Oftentimes my exit point once in the trade will be the two-day low, that is the lowest the price has been in the past two periods is the stop exit point. If I am especially confident, then it will be a three-period low.

HERE'S ONE I MADE EARLIER

Figure 4.6 illustrates an example of this strategy in action. Note where the stop loss is and how the pattern does indeed illustrate a turnaround in the price. It can be uncannily accurate. However, we still need a stop-loss for those occasions when it is not!

Figure 4.6   Price movements showing a good stop-loss point

Recipe 5
Moving Averages:
Decisions Decisions
Difficulty Level: Beginner

Average is a matter of perspective, and this year, average is looking pretty good
—Scott Pattee

HISTORY OF THE RECIPE

Moving averages come in various forms, but their underlying purpose remains the same: to help technical traders track the trends of financial assets by smoothing out the day-to-day price fluctuations, or noise.

J.M. Hurst, an aerospace engineer of 1970 vintage, saw something about stock market data that nobody else had been able to see: that a stock price history was not a record of a continuously changing price, but a profile of a discrete sequence of individual magnitudes related to each other by a common wedge of time. That little thought experiment made a simple moving average analogous to a digital filter that could slice stock price history into bins of frequency, amplitude and phase and, when desired, numerically recombine them into the everyday stock chart. However, the way they are used in most trading textbooks means they are too late and inaccurate to give valid trading signals.

INGREDIENTS

All you need is web charting or charting software which allows you to add both **simple moving average (SMA)** and **exponential moving average (EMA)**.

There are other types of moving average but these two will suffice for what we will be doing.

Moving averages work in all time frames and generally across all markets. They do not work in the most illiquid ones, and certainly they are no good for stocks that have recently entered the markets, i.e. initial public offerings (IPOs).

RECIPE

Simple Moving Average (SMA)

Look for the set up shown in Figure 5.1.

- **(A)** From beginning of 2004 we were long on the S&P 500 Energy Sector.
- **(B)** Stopped out on 23 January 2008 on decisive break of 200-day SMA.
- **(C)** We had an opportunity to go short on the S&P 500 Energy Sector on the crossing of the 200-day SMA by our signal line – the 50-day SMA.
- **(D)** Tail end of 2010 we have another signal to go long

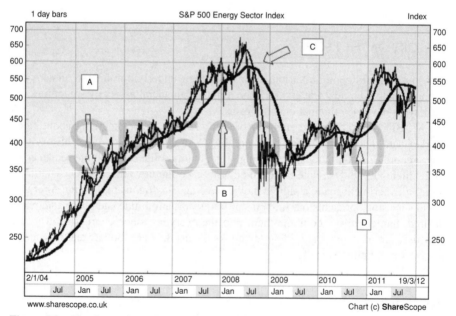

Figure 5.1   Simple moving average on S&P 500 chart
Source: www.sharescope.co.uk. © ShareScope, reproduced with permission

Simple moving averages work best in pairs. The example shown in Figure 5.1 is a typical professional set up where both the 200 SMA and the 50 SMA (which is always closer to the price) are displayed to indicate a high possibility of a change in trend. Normally the shorter time frame is the signal line and dictates where the market may be heading.

If you know the general direction of the trend then as long as the market stays above the longer term SMA (200 SMA in this example) we should be looking to go **long above the line and short below the line**.

Cooking Tip: Each time the market touches the long-term SMA, we should be ready to go either long or short.

The skill is in knowing where the stop is. This is normally sought at the point where we know we are wrong, i.e. when the market moves aggressively through both lines. You must allow for market noise. As you can see in 2006 we could have been stopped twice, and as has been discussed we normally should look to exit at a point $2 \times$ ATR from the trend line, i.e. the 200 SMA.

This could be quite expensive for long-term trading, but as you can see the profits can be substantial. What we will discuss now is the shorter term signals.

VARIATIONS TO THE RECIPE

Large professional trading companies use a combination of SMAs and EMAs. A typical combination is the 24 SMA and the 10 EMA. The EMA acts as an indicator that will hug the price up or down. The SMA is used as a place to be stopped should the market trade through it. This is best illustrated with the AUDUSD forex cross as shown in Figure 5.2.

The EMA **weighs current prices more heavily than past prices**. This gives the EMA the advantage of being quicker to respond to price fluctuations than an SMA; however, that can also be viewed as a disadvantage because the EMA is more prone to whipsaws (i.e. false signals).

Points to note:

- 10-period EMA hugs the price; the **SMA will always lag the price**
- Stops are placed at $2 \times$ ATR from the SMA line, so usually you are not whipped out of positions
- This does not work at all well in sideways markets, e.g. between 12pm and 7pm (in Figure 5.2)

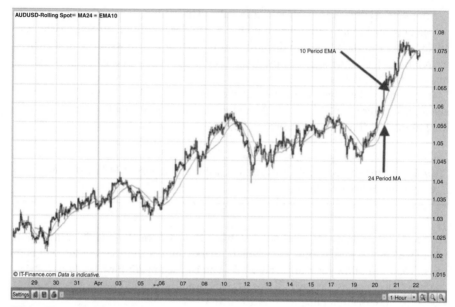

Figure 5.2 AUDUSD rolling spot
Source: © Sterlingmarkets.com, reproduced with permission

MORE ON THE RECIPE

Moving averages should be used as part of an arsenal of tools and ingredients to spice up and confirm the direction of the market, whether sideways, up or down.

For your reference other moving averages include:

- adaptive moving average
- triangular moving average
- typical price moving average (pivot point)
- weighted moving average (WMA)

HERE'S ONE I MADE EARLIER

50 and 200 SMA

We had been trying to get into Apple for some time and following some basic rules we had our first opportunity midway through 2009. The market was improving after the credit crunch and we knew Steve Jobs was a manager we wanted to invest in. Apple Computer Inc. finally gave us a chance to be in a winning trade we have held since 2009. We used only the 50-day and 200-day SMAs for our long-term trade. See Figure 5.3.

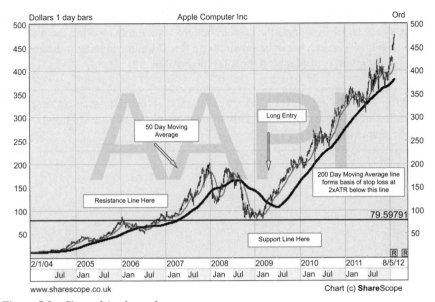

Figure 5.3   Chart of Apple stock
Source: www.sharescope.co.uk. © ShareScope, reproduced with permission

We did not use moving averages independently but added the support/resistance lines in for comfort and also learned about the management.

10 EMA and 14 SMA

A two-day GBPUSD chart is shown in Figure 5.4, which allows us to use the 10 EMA and the 14-day SMA. The basic theory is that the larger the gap between the

Figure 5.4   Price chart of GBP/USD
Source: © Sterlingmarkets.com, reproduced with permission

two lines and if a reversal is seen then we should take the signal. The gap between the SMA and the EMA signals the need to be more diligent in entering the market.

The stop is placed at a break below or above the SMA, the lagging indicator line, but some discretion is needed as to how far the break is.

Cooking Tip: The greater the gap between the signal line and the EMA is a good indication of increased volatility. This strategy works best in steady trends with little real volatility.

Recipe 6
Breakfast at 8

Difficulty Level: Beginner

Hope is a good breakfast but a bad supper.

—Francis Bacon

HISTORY OF THE RECIPE

The first hour normally sets the tone for the day in many markets. This is the same strategy that was used by Paresh when he was trading the Japanese Government Bond (JGB) contract on LIFFE (London International Financial Futures and Options Exchange), from 1994 to 1997. The JGB at the time was the largest contract tradable on LIFFE. This means that a single tick movement whether up or down (where tick is the smallest point movement from say 141.72 to 141.73 could mean a trading account gaining or losing approximately £145.

From Wikipedia we learn:

> Herd mentality describes how people are influenced by their peers to adopt certain behaviors, follow trends, and/or purchase items. Examples of the herd mentality include stock market trends, fashions in apparel, cars, taste in music, home décor, etc. Social psychologists study the related topics of group intelligence, crowd wisdom, and decentralized decision making.

In no other area is this more prevalent than the stock markets where the herd mentality is personified, even for a limited time period, which gives strength to the strategy.

INGREDIENTS

An alarm clock to wake you up in time for the market to open, and a timer to ring at the end of one full hour of trading. Most charting packages will want you to pay exchange fees to get real-time prices, as a 15-minute delay will not do. Trading platforms like www.sterlingmarkets.com provide the basic recipe utensils you need in real time.

RECIPE

Breakfast at 7:00am or 8:00am?

The markets open at either 7:00 or 8:00 in the morning, depending on market and location. You need to decide in which market you wish to trade and be up in time for the market to open. The typical market will have created a range in the first hour and the usual set up is discussed below. In the first hour of trading, as shown in Figure 6.1, the Daily Rolling Future contract had made a range of 5955 to 5930.

Notice how you had to have patience as the first trade opportunity was not available until 10:30am. As you can tell, all we wait for is the breakout of the first hour's trading.

Figure 6.1   UK 100 Daily Rolling Future
Source: © Sterlingmarkets.com, reproduced with permission

Our stop is the high or the low of the day depending if we are going long or short. In this example we went short. Of course with 24-hour trading becoming more prevalent it does make it harder to execute. The best way to play this strategy is to stick to the market time zones you work in for your local market.

VARIATIONS TO THE RECIPE

The German Bund opens at 7:00am UK time. This clearly shows why you cannot just trade the breakout of an hourly range. From Figure 6.2 we can see that the first break, short, came back within the hourly range identified by the horizontal trend lines drawn between 120.665 and 120.79. We had another opportunity to go long at about 08:45a.m. where again the price broke out of our hourly range.

Cooking Tip: Fixed income has been the best follower of this trade from experience. There is no reason why in the above example you go short at 08:15 and take profit, then go long at 08:45. This does limit you to trading twice a day max.

Figure 6.2   2-minute Bund chart
Source: www.eSignal.com

MORE ON THE RECIPE

This strategy is really good for beginners who do not wish to be inundated with indicators and complexities that may require a statistics degree to understand. The concept is simple, after the first hour you can be sure that any rounding of positions by traders and institutions larger than us overnight will have finished. The rest of the day is all about the battle between buyers and sellers, that is demand and supply.

Since our objective is to just add hard cash to our trading account day in day out we MUST have stops and targets.

No complicated charting package is required, just the detail of the most recent high and low for the day.

The skill is having discipline, which instils the correct money management for this trade set up. Do not risk more than 2% of the capital on any single day. If your account is opened with £10,000 then look to lose only £200. This means you should be looking to make £200 or more for the day also.

Trades of this type typically do not fall in the category of having the perfect risk/reward ratio.

Cooking Tip: Make five ticks per breakout. As you get a feel for how the market behaves, you may increase this. On first breakout STOP is at the other extreme of hourly range! Invariably you need to stick to the £200 loss and stop trading.

HERE'S ONE I MADE EARLIER

Example 1

Figure 6.3 shows the Wall Street DOW rolling cash on 10 February 2012. Range for hour was 12744 – 12794. Entered long trade after 20:59 on same day and was filled at 12796 and exited at 12804 on close of the market at 21:15. An eight-point gain only on this occasion and as you can see you have to have patience to trade using this strategy.

The point here is that we are looking to just bag the cash. This will help build confidence and understanding of market activity.

Example 2

More recently we used this strategy on the German Bund, which, from Figure 6.4, clearly shows a range-bound market in the first hour between 13760 and 13800. The initial break of the high proved to be a false break and although we were in the trade our stop was at the day's low. We had to practice some patience and wait for the market to continue in the desired direction after about a 2.5 hour wait. We closed at

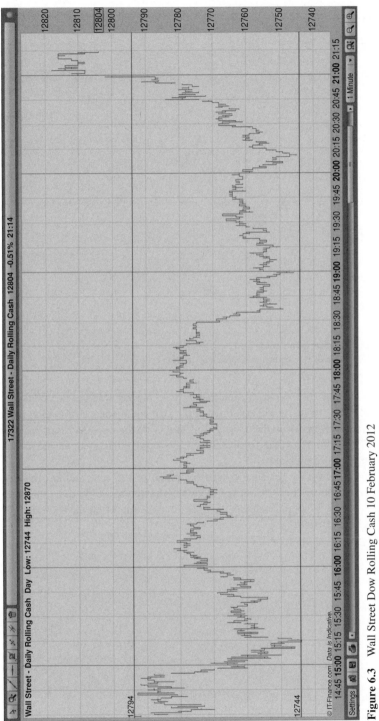

Figure 6.3 Wall Street Dow Rolling Cash 10 February 2012

Source: © Sterlingmarkets.com, reproduced with permission

Figure 6.4   5-minute Bund chart
Source: © Sterlingmarkets.com, reproduced with permission

the end of the day in good profit. On this day the market was not as volatile as the previous example as increased volatility implies an equal chance of market reversal.

In this trade we employed the trailing stop facility on the www.sterlingmarkets.com platform. The trailing stop was fixed at 5 ticks above the initial breakout and the market never returned to stop us out.

As with all things, experience counts for much of the 'gut feeling' that traders often speak of. On this occasion it was knowing that a reasonably quiet morning can continue – or if a breakout happens we must give the market some room in order to make maximum benefit.

Recipe 7
Let's Get a Takeaway!
Difficulty Level: Beginner

The secret to being successful from a trading perspective is to have an indefatigable and an undying and unquenchable thirst for information and knowledge.

—Paul Tudor Jones, Hedge Fund Manager

HISTORY OF THE RECIPE

What if a website could supply you with trading signals instead of you having to look for them? That is, you don't do the cooking, someone else does it for you – as in a takeaway. What if it automatically drew where the price is anticipated to go, so all you had to do was enter the order? Share prices often move in certain patterns. History suggests when these patterns will occur, that is the prices, with reasonable accuracy, will hit certain targets. How do we know this? Well over decades stock junkies have analysed hundreds of patterns and come to some conclusions. They give these patterns names, such as 'head and shoulders', and they set rules based on these patterns as to where the price is forecasted to go.

Figure 7.1 shows an example of a 'falling wedge' price move, which automatically generates the anticipated price move.

'A' is the range the price is expected to reach. It is shaded in the figure.

'B' is the initial minimum expected forecast the price is expected to reach.

'C' is the breakout – where the price moves through a resistance line, i.e. a line where the price has tended to touch then bounce back down from. When it breaks through we expect momentum and price trends to continue.

Throughout history many strategies have been developed which have used the concept that all the information is already in the price – and prices will

Figure 7.1   A falling wedge price move
Source: © Sterlingmarkets.com, reproduced with permission

follow patterns that occur due to the emotions of the investing and trading community.

> Technical analysis is perhaps the oldest device designed to beat the market. It has a secular history given that its origins can be traced to the seminal articles published by Charles H. Dow in the *Wall Street Journal* between 1900 and 1902, and its basic concepts became popular after contributions by Hamilton (1922) and Rhea (1932). A complete jargon of words and pictures has been developed since then and many traders, nowadays, take their buying and selling decisions on the basis of technical analysis results appearing on their screen.
>
> —Cesari and Crimonini (2003)

Figures 7.2 and 7.3 show how price chart patterns sometimes indicate a higher than random probability of the price subsequently moving in a particular direction. The initial target price, and the shaded area are in the range to be hit by the security that is anticipated by the pattern.

A lot of chart patterns centre around a breakout of the price. That is when a price moves beyond a resistance line and so the odds are in favour of a new trend having been established. See, for example, Figure 7.4.

INGREDIENTS

On this occasion we will be looking only at the technological advances that have now made it possible to pick our favourite patterns, display them for any market of

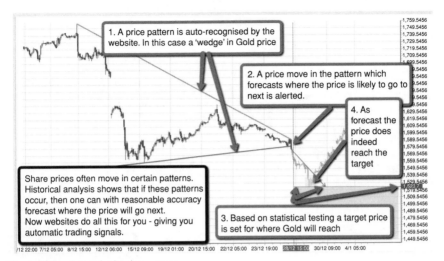

Figure 7.2 A 'wedge' price pattern

Source: © Sterlingmarkets.com, reproduced with permission

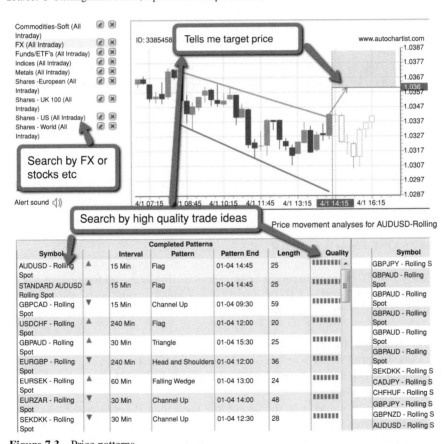

Figure 7.3 Price patterns

Source: www.tradermindmarkets.com

Figure 7.4   Price breakout

interest and tell us what the trade entry and stop-loss will be. As with any 'takeout' we can then pick and choose our favourite market and pattern and literally just apply the dressing – i.e. the amount we want to risk on the trade!

RECIPE

To explain this strategy we just need to pick up the menu from our trading platform. In this case we are using www.tradermindmarkets.com.

HERE'S ONE I MADE EARLIER

So does it work? Do the patterns forecast the price? How many trades, had we placed them, would have worked? To answer these questions, we did an experiment. We looked at gold patterns, which had come up on the site, and the targets. Our strategy is:

1. Buy when the chart pattern indicates to buy.
2. Sell at the price target or stop-loss, whichever is hit first.
3. The stop-loss is set at the same level from the entry as the profit, but in the opposite direction of course.
4. If your stop-loss is hit, you should not lose more than 2% of your overall capital and so your trade size should be set accordingly. For example, if you have $10,000. You should not lose more than $200 on a single trade (i.e. 2% of $10,000).

You may wonder: why should I not let the trade run until the profit target is hit? The answer is: imagine you have 100 trades, and on the winning one, you make $100. You have 60 winning trades, then you have $6,000 profit. If you have 40 losing trades, then you have a $4,000 loss if each was a loss of $100. But what if you didn't set a stop-loss? Then you could easily exceed the $6,000 gains.

Now, you ask, what if my stop-loss is $150? Fine, but then your profits are razor thin or completely wiped out.

Then you think some more and say, what if my profit target is set further away, so I make more than $100? The problem with that is chart patterns are based on likely targets. Just because you want the price to move more does not mean that historical statistical experience suggests it will.

Okay, what if you bet more money on each trade so instead of making $100 when you hit the profit target you make $200? Again, that's fine, but you don't know ahead of time which are winning trades and which are losing trades, so your losses also increase. Of course your overall profit doubles. But then you have to think, what if you have five losing trades in a row? It can and does happen. If you lose $200 × 5 then that is $1,000 lost. That is fine if you had $10,000 starting capital as it is only 10% after five trades. But if you made the error of losing that much with much less trading capital, e.g. $1,000, then you are wiped out anyway.

I mention this not because I want you to not make money, but because it comes from years of professional hedge fund experience. And not a single professional fund manager would contradict me.

Figure 7.5 illustrates a winning trade.

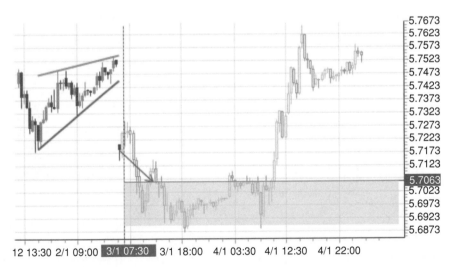

Figure 7.5   USD/DKK: winning trade
Source: © Sterlingmarkets.com, reproduced with permission

Figure 7.6   NZD/JPY: failed trade
Source: © Sterlingmarkets.com, reproduced with permission

Figure 7.6 shows a failed trade. If entry is 60.24 and profit target is 60.06 (i.e. 0.18 points) then the stop-loss exit is 60.24 + 0.18 (i.e. 60.42). The stop-loss is hit before the target is hit. So this is a failed trade.

A successful trade is shown in Figure 7.7.

Figure 7.7   NZD/JPY: successful trade
Source: © Sterlingmarkets.com, reproduced with permission

Figure 7.8 AUD/JPY: winning trade
Source: © Sterlingmarkets.com, reproduced with permission

Figures 7.8 and 7.9 show more winning trades.

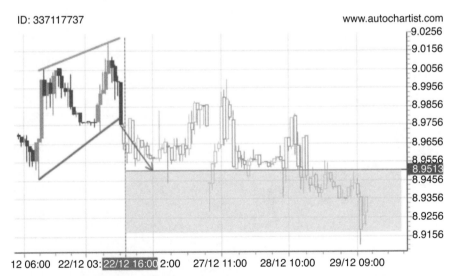

Figure 7.9 EUR/SEK: winning trade
Source: © Sterlingmarkets.com, reproduced with permission

Figure 7.10   EUR/CAD: failed trade
Source: © Sterlingmarkets.com, reproduced with permission

In Figure 7.10, a failed trade, the profit target is hit well after the stop-loss.
Figures 7.11 and 7.12 provide further examples of winning trades.

Figure 7.11   USD/DKK: winning trade
Source: © Sterlingmarkets.com, reproduced with permission

Figure 7.12   AUD/CHF: winning trade
Source: © Sterlingmarkets.com, reproduced with permission

In Figure 7.13 the trade narrowly misses hitting the profit target, then narrowly hits the stop-loss, which would be around 0.8258.

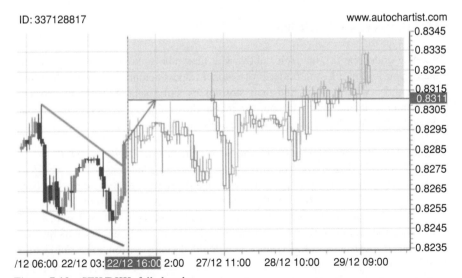

Figure 7.13   SEK/DKK: failed trade
Source: © Sterlingmarkets.com, reproduced with permission

Figure 7.14   USD/JPY: winning trade
Source: © Sterlingmarkets.com, reproduced with permission

Figure 7.14 shows a winning trade, albeit small.

Conclusion: 7 out of 10 winning trades – albeit a very small sample. That's not a bad result at all. And given the time one saves in finding trades, it is clear to see why a 'takeaway' is more attractive than cooking dinner ourselves.

VARIATIONS ON THE RECIPE

Of course under the original rules above you make the same amount in a winning trade as you lose in a losing trade. Professional traders actually are better than that. They let those winners run. And their stop-losses will not be as far away. So let's look at spicing up and improving our original trading recipe to be more professional.

First, how do you let winners run? Here are some sample rules:

1. Once the initial price target is hit, you double the position size and exit if:
    a. the price moves to the lowest it's been in the immediate past two periods
    b. it moves from the peak against you, twice the normal average range it's been trading in each period over the last, say, 10 periods. For example if the range from high to low in each bar for the past 10 periods is 5, 6, 4, 3, 7, 5, 6, 4, 3, 7 then the average is 5. So as soon as the price moves 10 points from its high (or low if it was a short trade) since you doubled your position you would exit.
2. What about tighter stop-losses so we lose less? A clever place to put a stop-loss is under the 'breakout' resistance line, i.e. a place the price should not go if the breakout is valid (see Figure 7.15).

Figure 7.15 A trade set up based on a price chart breakout pattern
Source: © Sterlingmarkets.com, reproduced with permission

Of course a tighter stop-loss will change the win–loss ratio, but should make your winning trades more profitable when combined with a rule that lets winning trades run. But some people like to keep things simple.

RESOURCES

www.investingbetter.com – educational videos on trading.

www.tradermindmarkets.com – a site offering automatic patterns as identified in this chapter.

www.sharescope.co.uk/alpesh – software allowing you to chart patterns.

Part II
HORS D'OEUVRES

The recipes for trading success in this section are for the beginner/intermediate level trader. By adding these to the mix, you open up your trading opportunities because they work equally well across all markets, from forex to commodities and equities, time frames, and for 1-minute to weekly charts.

> Hors d'oeuvres have always a pathetic interest for me; they remind me of one's childhood that one goes through wondering what the next course is going to be like – and during the rest of the menu one wishes one had eaten more of the hors d'oeuvres.
>
> —H.H. Munro (English novelist)

Recipe 8
MACD, MA and Stochastic – Mixing Cocktails
Difficulty Level: Beginner/Intermediate

The really important things are said over cocktails and are never done.
—Peter F. Drucker

HISTORY OF THE RECIPE

Stochastic implementation was developed from the very basics of particle theory, which was called the Brownian motion experiment. This, some may recall from their childhood, was all about the random nature of gases or liquids in the natural habitat – NATURE! It was discovered that, in certain circumstances, the natural course could be predicted to have a certain outcome under certain pressures. The stochastic oscillator was developed in the 1950s and is used to show the positioning of the current close relative to the high/low range of a market over a period of time.

INGREDIENTS

As before, you just need an adequate charting package, ShareScope or eSignal, and the various indicators should be set at their default.

- **Stochastic.** This indicator helps to highlight extreme movements in price. By itself, it works exceptionally well in ranging markets showing what markets may be overbought or oversold – but fails when markets trend.
- **MACD.** MACD is very useful for establishing whether a market is still in a trend or will continue a trend. Therefore the weakness of only using stochastic is negated by

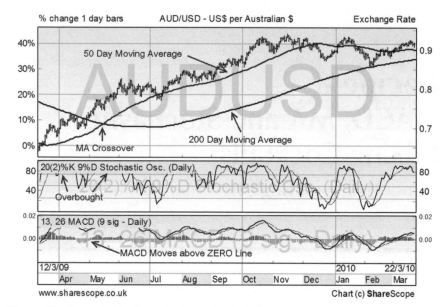

Figure 8.1 Example of using only the stochastic indicator
Source: www.sharescope.co.uk. © ShareScope, reproduced with permission

adding MACD to the mix. When using MACD in conjunction with other indicators we **only** look at the MACD histogram.

- **Moving average.** Those most commonly used by professionals are the 50- and 200-day moving averages.

RECIPE

Knowing the settings is one thing, you must also be aware of how the indicator reacts in live markets. Figure 8.1 explains clearly that the stochastic indicator alone is not to be trusted. The Australian currency is clearly in an uptrend, and yet the stochastic indicator keeps us guessing if this is truly overbought.

From March 2009 to October 2009 the currency moved up 42.5%. This is the magic of having a checklist that you literally tick boxes to keep you in a trade for the longer term. Let me explain the set up, which will become your checklist for May 2009.

COOKING CHECKLIST

Moving average – Is the market above the 50-day moving average, or has it just moved above the 50-day moving average? Check

Stochastic – Is the indicator still close to overbought signal line 80? Check

MACD – Is the histogram moving above the zero line? Check

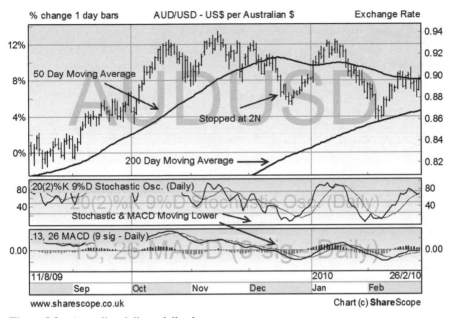

Figure 8.2 Australian dollar – daily chart
Source: www.sharescope.co.uk. © ShareScope, reproduced with permission

Having checked these attributes in May 2009, we could have ridden the market all the way up with a stop at 2N below the 50-day moving average (see Figure 8.2). But that is not the end of it. What happened is remarkable as we entered the market in May 2009 at 0.748 and we stopped at 0.881 in December 2009, achieving a total gain of **19.7%**.

As with the old saying: two heads are better than one. It follows that two to three indicators are far superior to a single one.

Cooking Tip: Try not to mix too many indicators together – generally three is fine with a specific exit strategy for these longer term trades like 2N where N is the average true range.

VARIATIONS TO THE RECIPE

If we can go long using this strategy it follows that we must be able to go short also. The EUR/USD trade shown in Figure 8.3 is a good example of our checklist in reverse.

Figure 8.3   US dollar per euro trade
Source: www.sharescope.co.uk. © ShareScope, reproduced with permission

---

COOKING CHECKLIST

Moving average – Is the market still below or moved **below** the 50-day moving
  average? Check
Stochastic – Is the indicator still close to the oversold signal line 20? Check
MACD – Is the histogram moving below the zero line? Check

Where we need to be cautious is not to take false signals. We are looking for the
stochastic to stay either in the overbought or the oversold area, not move aggressively
away from it. This bodes well for longer term trade actually forming a long-term
trend. Our entry and exit is the length of the vertical line: that is we have a total gain
of **9.6%** again using 2N above the 50-day moving average as our stop!

MORE ON THE RECIPE

This system set up works exceptionally well for the longer term technical analyst. It
can be used for shorter term time scales and the sugar trade shown in Figure 8.4 on a
15-minute chart is a good example.

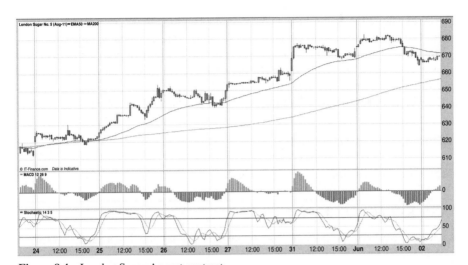

Figure 8.4 London Sugar August contract
Source: © Sterlingmarkets.com, reproduced with permission

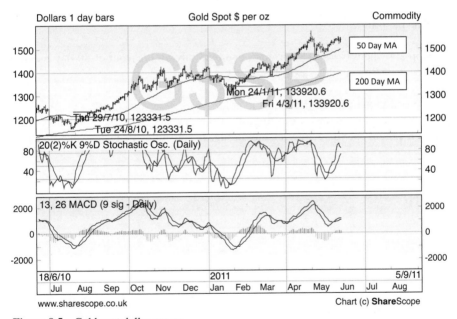

Figure 8.5 Gold spot dollar per oz
Source: www.sharescope.co.uk. © ShareScope, reproduced with permission

On 26 May 2011 as the MACD histogram moved to above the zero line and the stochastic was still above or close to the overbought area, we entered on a breakout of the 50-period moving average and we exited as per normal on a breakout to the downside by a factor of 2N, where N is now the average price range for 15 minutes. We exited at the end of the day on 1 June 2011.

You have to be exceptionally diligent for false breakouts on smaller time frames.

HERE'S ONE I MADE EARLIER

Figure 8.5 shows an example of trading gold.

COOKING CHECKLIST

Moving average – Is the market still above the 50-day moving average ENTRY 1233? Check

Stochastic – Is the 24 August 2010 indicator still close to overbought signal line 80? Check

MACD – Is the 24 August MACD histogram above the zero line? Check

---

Note the following:

- Stop 2N where N = ATR for gold, and exit only on breakout of 50-day moving average at 2N – in this case 1339.

There is a total gain of 106 points in gold.

We stayed with the trade from August 2010 to January 2011. Note that this can tie up your capital but you can tweak the settings to something that suits your appetite.

Recipe 9
The Breakout
Difficulty Level: Intermediate

It was a good game. It was a step in the right direction. But I don't know if breakout game is appropriate.

—Chris Chambers

HISTORY OF THE RECIPE

This is a simple trading strategy that works because it incorporates great trading practice and principles. It exemplifies what makes a good recipe into a profitable dish by including the correct measure of risk/reward and the discipline not to overcook a trade so that losses become larger. It is also the strategy I prefer beyond all others because it clearly shows entry and exit.

The strategy works on the basis that a price with momentum will continue in that direction (see Figure 9.1).

- Find a trend, e.g. downward trend (1)
- Locate a breakout from that trend to the upside (2) as a purchase point. Enter when the high of the breakout price bar is exceeded
- Set a stop-loss, i.e. know when you are wrong, e.g. price resumes downward trend (3)
- Set a profit target based on a reasonable recent price level (4) but exit if the price moves to the lowest it's been in, say, the last three periods (see below for more explanation on this)
- Ensure reward target (Reward – Entry) is greater than risk (Entry – Stop-loss) (i.e. $(4 - 2) > (2 - 3)$)

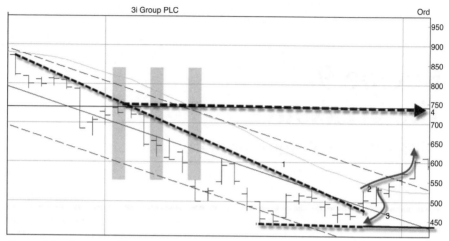

Figure 9.1   Downtrend for 3i Group PLC
Data taken from ShareScope

- Trade size should be such that the amount you could lose is less than 2% of total portfolio value, i.e. $2\% < (2 - 3)$
- Aggressive: if price is halfway between entry and profit target, then double stake and move stop-loss to entry price

INGREDIENTS

- Rules
- Price charting software or website

RECIPE

Entry

1. Find a trend and a breakout from that trend.

Exit

2. Set a profit level greater than a stop-loss level. The stop-loss should be the point beneath the trend line, where if the price returns we would know we were wrong in the trade, i.e. if a breakout is genuine, then the price should stay above the trend line in the direction of the breakout.
3. If markets are random and have an equal chance of moving up or down, i.e. 50–50, then it stands to reason that if your profit targets are ALWAYS greater than your stop loss targets, you should be profitable.

Money Management

Amount to bet: the maximum loss should not be more than 2% of your trading capital.

VARIATIONS TO THE RECIPE

The initial exit is the stop-loss and is set at where the price should not move if you are correct, namely back beneath the trend line. After that I tend to exit at a three-day low of the price, i.e. the lowest the price has been in three days.

HERE'S ONE I MADE EARLIER

The trade shown in Figure 9.2 did not work out. You can see where I thought the breakout was, but the next day the price moves even higher suggesting an entry. Then it drops back below the downtrend and hits the stop-loss.

Figure 9.3 shows another trade from the same trading series that did not work. Now the important thing to learn is that:

1. The stop-loss is quick to kick in with this strategy so you don't have to wait long to find out.
2. There is no point arguing if the downtrend line and the breakout price should have been 1 mm here or there. Instead draw the best line you can. You will forever be drawing lines and not trading if you try moving them around by a millimetre here or there.

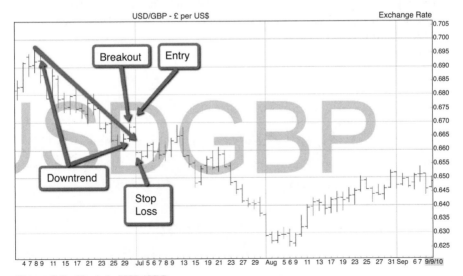

Figure 9.2   Trade in USD/GBP
Data taken from www.sterlingmarkets.com

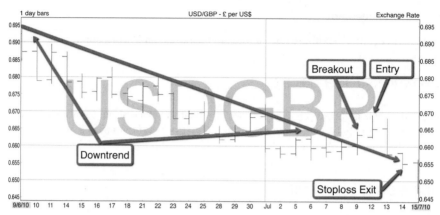

Figure 9.3 Losing trade in USD/GBP
Data taken from www.sterlingmarkets.com

Figure 9.4 shows a trade that worked.

And Figure 9.5 provides a close-up image of the above.

Notice that the high of the breakout bar was not broken until a few days later, and that was the entry point.

- The entry in the above would be 0.632.
- I set the exit at 0.660 because that is a recent price level that has already been hit. The reward would therefore be 0.0280 points (or in forex language, 280 pips). This type of trade is not restricted to forex of course.
- The stop-loss initially was set at below the downtrend. That would be approximately around 0.624. So the loss from entry if it did go to stop-loss would have been 0.632 – 0.620, that is 0.120 points.

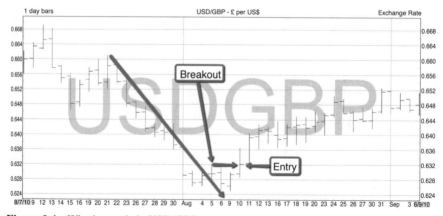

Figure 9.4 Winning trade in USD/GBP
Data taken from www.sterlingmarkets.com

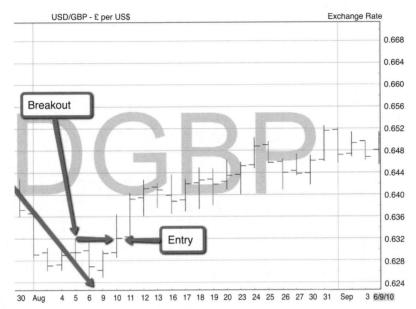

Figure 9.5   Close up of winning USD/GBP trade
Data taken from www.sterlingmarkets.com

So my potential reward is greater than my potential loss and that makes this a trade worth doing.

SOME RECIPE QUESTIONS

Q.   How long do I wait once the breakout has occurred for the price to move above the breakout bar's high?

A.   You will notice in Figure 9.5 that the breakout bar and the entry point were three days apart. That is because the price did not move above the breakout bar's high price until then. Three days, or periods, is fine – even five. But I would not leave it longer than that as the original force of the breakout tends to have gone by then.

Q.   How do you set a profit target? Or: When is it time to take it out of the oven?

A.   In the above example I picked a recent price high. How do you pick one? It is an art. The level has to be something the price has reached in the recent past. We work on the basis that if it has recently been there, then it can reasonably reach it again in the same time frame. This is not 100% guaranteed, but it is a sensible way of setting a target.

Q.   What do you mean, 'the lowest it has been in three periods, or a three-day low'?

A.   See Figure 9.6.

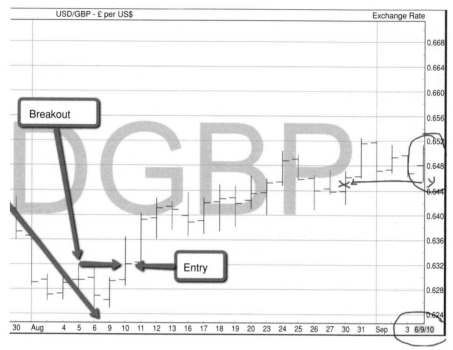

Figure 9.6 Explaining targets
Data taken from www.sterlingmarkets.com

Imagine we entered correctly at the point marked 'Entry'. And imagine today is 6/9/10, which I have circled. I have also circled the price bar for today. I have written 'y' at what is the low point of price for that day. Note that it is the lowest price for five days. Basically look at 'x', where the price has entered into the price range from five days ago. It is therefore the lowest it's been in three days (since five days are more than three days!) and so we exit.

Take a look at the price on the previous trading day to 6/9/10. There the lowest the price hits is about where it was two days prior to that. Therefore not a three-day low and so we don't exit. Why do I pick a 'three-day low'? Because it is usually a good trick to know when prices are changing direction and we may well want to get out.

I show this in more detail in Figure 9.7.

Q.   Why does the reward have to be greater than the loss?
A.   Because imagine we are right and wrong 50% of the time. If reward was not greater than loss then we would simply break even. We would make as much as we lose unless when we won, we won more than what we lose, when we lose.
Q.   Why do I have to wait for a breakout? Why can't I just pick a target which is greater than a stop-loss exit? Then even if the market moves up 50% of the time and down 50% of the time, I still make money – as in Figure 9.8. Here I enter

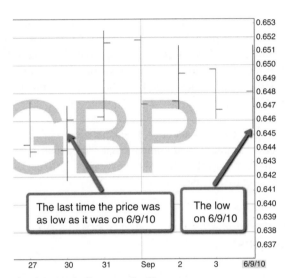

Figure 9.7 Zooming in to trade for more detail
Data taken from www.sterlingmarkets.com

at 1.5519. I set a profit target of +7 and a stop-loss of −5. I do 10 more of these trades on other stocks. Surely then I am diversified and if 5 of my 10 trades make money and 5 of them lose money, then I am up?

A. It's a neat idea. And as well as giving you a theoretical answer I will give you a real practical one too. This would work if there was a 50% chance of a +7 and

Figure 9.8 Setting the targets for profit and loss
Data taken from www.sterlingmarkets.com

a –5 move (ignore commissions and buy/sell spreads for now). But that is not the case. In reality the probability of a +5 and –5 is the same (all things being equal, i.e. no trend in place etc.). And the probability of a +7 and –7 is also the same. But the probability of a +7 is less than a –5. So you more often hit a –5 than a +7. Our outcome would be to breakeven in this scenario (ignoring commissions).

That is why we look for a breakout. A breakout represents price momentum. It is conceptually agreed amongst professionals that a breakout increases the odds in our favour to be right more often than we are wrong. This epiphany comes with experience and sticking to the rules.

WHAT COULD GO WRONG? HOW MIGHT YOU END UP OVERCOOKING THIS?

The usual problem is lack of discipline in executing the strategy. Traders, out of fear, take a profit too early or don't take the loss when they are supposed to. That ruins the mathematics behind the strategy. Traders convince themselves when it comes time to exit at a loss, that if only they hold on, then things will turn around. And sometimes they do. But the problem is the underlying mathematics behind the returns is then disrupted and you may get lucky once, but when luck runs out, you end up losing money.

Part III
AMUSE-BOUCHE

These strategies are for the intermediate level trader, albeit they are not very complicated, but they do add to the sophistication of the strategies so far described. For instance by adding volume with breakouts we are increasing the odds of calling the markets correctly.

> The predinner treat known as an amuse-bouche, or amuse-gueule used to be a throwaway, a complimentary palate pleaser, to translate the term, which was put before the diner to make a good impression. Recently, however, like a bit player with big ideas, it has begun to hog the stage.
> —William Grimes (*New York Times* journalist)

Recipe 10
Natural Diet: Don't Forget Your Roughage
Difficulty Level: Intermediate

The four most dangerous words in investing are 'This time it's different'.

—Sir John Templeton

HISTORY OF THE RECIPE

Leonardo Fibonacci, or, more commonly, simply Fibonacci, was an Italian mathematician, considered by some as the most talented western mathematician of the Middle Ages.

Fibonacci is best known to the modern world for disseminating the Hindu–Arabic numeral system in Europe, primarily through the publication in the early 13th century of his *Book of Calculation*, the *Liber Abaci*; and for a number sequence named after him known as the *Fibonacci numbers*, which he did not discover but used as an example in the *Liber Abaci*.

But how did Fibonacci help with market trading? In mathematics, the Fibonacci numbers are a sequence of numbers where each number is the sum of the previous two numbers, starting with 0 and 1. This sequence begins 0, 1, 1, 2, 3, 5, 8, 13, 21, 34, 55, 89, 144, 233, 377, 610, 987 . . . . The higher up in the sequence, the closer two consecutive Fibonacci numbers of the sequence, divided by each other, will approach the golden ratio (approximately 1:1.618 or 0.618:1) to create the commonly known *golden spiral*. See Figure 10.1.

If we take a specific arc and divide it by the diameter, it will give us a specific ratio, 1.618. See Figure 10.2.

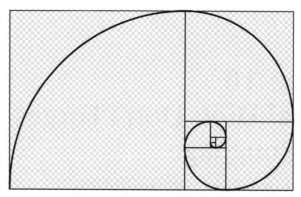

Figure 10.1   The golden spiral

Figure 10.2   Sea shell example of the golden ratio

This pattern can be found throughout nature and as a result can be applied to markets which are all governed to a greater or lesser extent by human nature.

INGREDIENTS

All you need is web charting or charting software, which allows you to add Fibonacci retracements and extensions to charts in *varying* time scales. We show how the golden spiral in markets can be formulated graphically in Figure 10.3.

Now we just need to put into practice the meaning of actual Fibonacci lines as they are drawn in the charts (without paying attention to the pain our Italian mathematician went through deciphering some ancient Indian Code). It is nature's way!

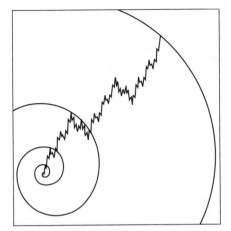

Figure 10.3 Graphical representation of the golden spiral in markets
Source: www. elliottwave.com

RECIPE

Look for the set up illustrated in Figure 10.4, remembering that, as this is related to nature, we must look to use this only on liquid markets which closely resemble mass psychology. In this example we will look at the US Nasdaq Futures contract.

In order to follow the direction of the expected trend shown in Figure 10.4, we use the Fibonacci Projection tool in the software. We draw the line from the extreme low to the extreme high, left to right on the most recent trend up, and then the software will find the relevant support/resistance lines according to the Fibonacci numbers. The key thing now is to know our entry and exit strategy.

Entry Signal

There are two basic entries:

1. Wait for the market to get close to the recent low, and buy with a stop 1N below the low, where N is the average true range in the market we are looking to trade. The reason for this is that the trend, if anticipated to be up, should not be making a new low, which implies the previous down trend is continuing.
2. Most likely we will enter the market on a new high, say at 1290, in Figure 10.4. This gives us confidence that the trend could well have changed and our stop can be placed below the current resistance (which should become support). As per usual we will use 2N as our stop below that line.

So we have an entry at 1290 where a new high will be made in Figure 10.4. The first target is 1555 as this is the first complete Fibonacci level/ratio of 1.618 (Figure 10.5).

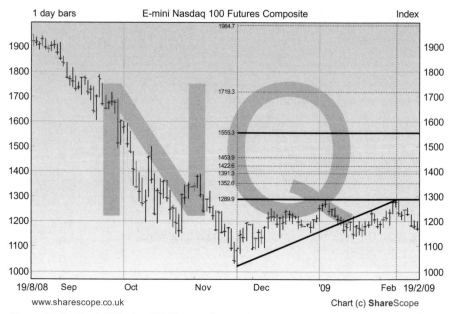

Figure 10.4   E-mini Nasdaq 100 Futures Composite
Source: www.sharescope.co.uk. © ShareScope, reproduced with permission

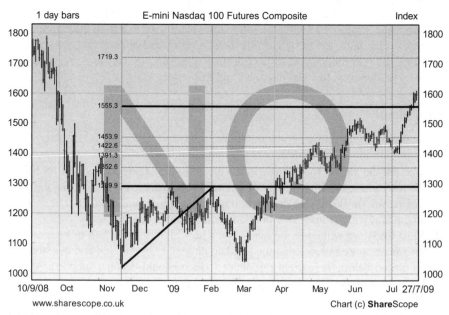

Figure 10.5   E-mini Nasdaq 100 Futures Composite – six months later
Source: www.sharescope.co.uk. © ShareScope, reproduced with permission

The results speak for themselves, when we fast forward the chart six months later (Figure 10.5).

Cooking Tip: Figure 10.5 shows a daily chart, and the same principle applies for smaller time scales. Each subdivided horizontal dotted line is expected to offer resistance and then support.

VARIATIONS TO THE RECIPE

The Fibonacci sequence is a natural phenomenon, and although fabulous at picking support and resistance, it really comes into its own when you can predict with certainty longer term targets as shown in Figure 10.6, bringing this market to recent times, where we far exceeded our initial target of 1555.

As with all indicators, they are not precise instruments, but you can clearly see just by predicting the bottom of the market in March 2009 and assessing the first leg up, we drew our Fibonacci Extension/Projection, and we had a forecast that the market was going to stall at around 2000 and then at 2400. This is valuable information when you have longer term goals in mind.

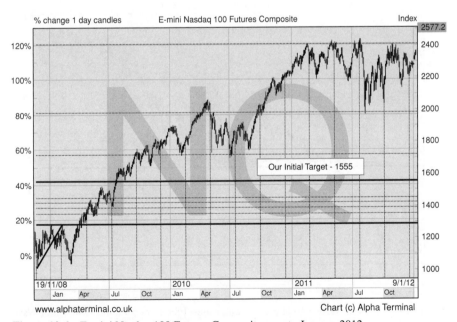

Figure 10.6   E-mini Nasdaq 100 Futures Composite – up to January 2012
Source: www.alphaterminal.co.uk. © Alpha Terminal, reproduced with permission

MORE ON THE RECIPE

We can think of Elliott wave theory and Fibonacci as cousins. When used together
they form a pretty strong alliance. If, in the same example of the Nasdaq, we were to
count the waves we would see that we may have been better prepared if we had used
the combined theories.

Figure 10.7 clearly shows the high in March 2011 is 2429 with a Fibonacci level
at 2411. Having counted five waves up on the major wave and five waves up on the
minor fifth wave (shown by the Roman numerals), we can with some confidence
suggest that the Nasdaq has indeed reached a prominent high and the market should
retrace to a lower Fibonacci level from the high of 2429. It followed that a short-term
top had formed and the market retraced back down to 1972.3 on 9 August 2011. We
applied the Fibonacci retracement tool again from the high in July 2011 (2411) to the
low in August 2011 (1972) – see Figure 10.8.

A major top materialised in July 2011, we used the Fibonacci tool to work out the
expected lower targets – in this case our initial target is 1876 as can be clearly seen
in Figure 10.8.

However, moving forward five months to January 2012, it was evident that this
short trade would have been stopped out – Figure 10.9.

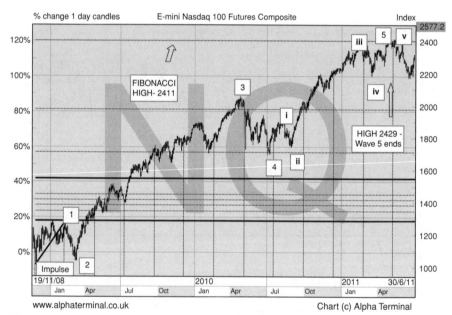

Figure 10.7 E-Mini Nasdaq 100 Futures Composite – Fibonacci combined with Elliot Wave
count
Source: www.alphaterminal.co.uk. © Alpha Terminal, reproduced with permission

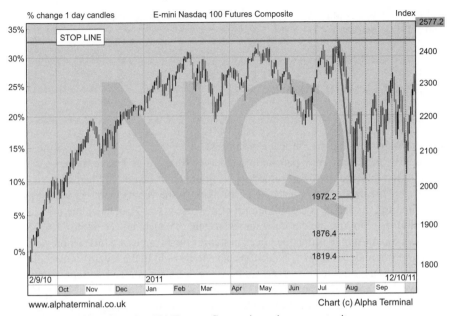

Figure 10.8   E-Mini Nasdaq 100 Futures Composite – short opportunity
Source: www.alphaterminal.co.uk. © Alpha Terminal, reproduced with permission

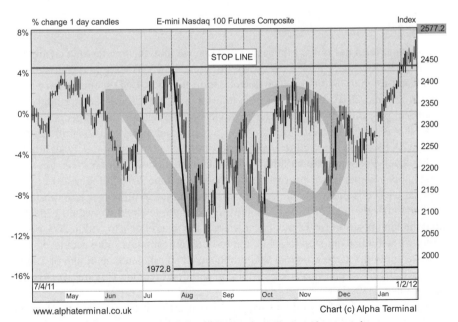

Figure 10.9   E-Mini Nasdaq 100 Futures Composite – short trade stopped out
Source: www.alphaterminal.co.uk. © Alpha Terminal, reproduced with permission

In conclusion: liquid and longer term horizons will give you the best levels to buy and sell in a market.

HERE'S ONE I MADE EARLIER

Example 1

For short-term trading the Fibonacci numbers can work. Figure 10.10 shows the chart of the GBP/USD currency pair and on a larger time frame I have picked a recent high. I then lowered my time frame to a 5-minute chart and on the first obvious five waves down I used the Fibonacci Tool to draw in the retracement. From this, and remembering my target is the full length of my first wave, I can calculate my target.

From top to bottom the currency moved a total of 111 points (1.6466 – 1.6355).

What you must note is that the prices in shorter time frames are much more volatile to your profit and loss (P&L). Your stops have to be tight to the level you have picked and the 111 target has to be worked out from the point where you have placed the end of Wave 2. So the real target is 1.6353 (i.e. 1.6464 – 0.0111 points). In Figure 10.11, you will notice that the market came close to wave 2 before heading south and hitting the target.

Example 2

For a longer term use of the Fibonacci numbers, we took the first leg of a significant rise in 2010 for the EUR/USD as shown in Figure 10.12. The art is in waiting for a significant trend to be broken. The downtrend in the EUR/USD seems to have been broken in June 2010. Waiting for a significant rise and retracement we apply the Fibonacci projection to take a longer term view on the market. Our target is 1.4980.

As this is a long-term strategy we have our stop below the most significant low of 1.1870, meaning we need to target our profit level at an appropriately significant higher level. Portfolios are built by having the dedication to your analysis. Let's see what happened moving fast forward from the low in June 2010 in Figure 10.13.

What we see is that we came very close to our target. With longer term positions we know that the market took 12 months to make the low and we would expect to hold the long position for 12 months at least. If the market gets to within 20% of our target we will raise our stop to 1.433, our most significant next Fibonacci level.

If we apply the same principle again to the most significant recent high of 1.4941 in April 2011, we can now look at this potential short trade (Figure 10.14). Our projection is 1.3070.

Again we can fast forward and see what has transpired (Figure 10.15). Here the market hit our target before the end of 2011, making this a very profitable two years of trading the EUR/USD currency.

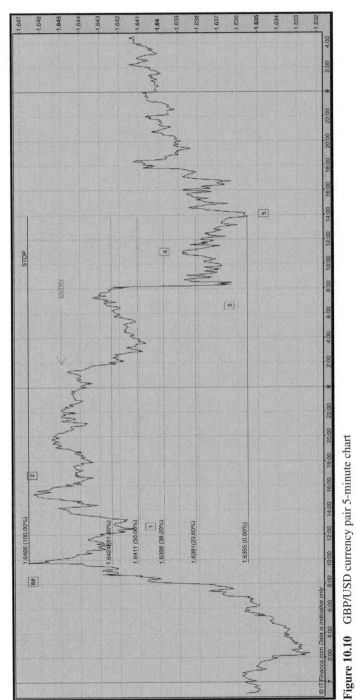

Figure 10.10 GBP/USD currency pair 5-minute chart
Source: © Sterlingmarkets.com, reproduced with permission

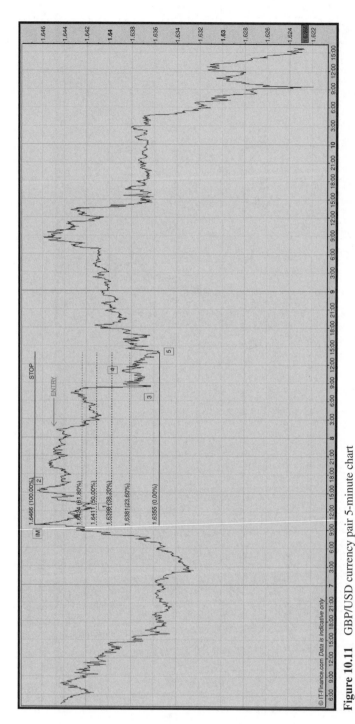

Figure 10.11 GBP/USD currency pair 5-minute chart

Source: © Sterlingmarkets.com, reproduced with permission

Figure 10.12   EUR/USD daily chart – long trade opportunity
Source: www.sharescope.co.uk. © ShareScope, reproduced with permission

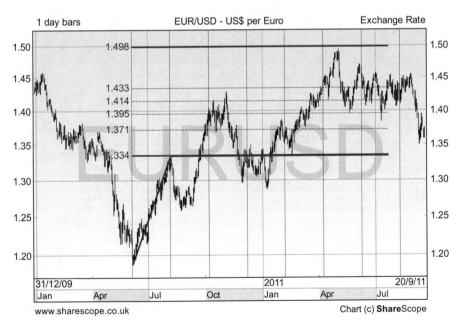

Figure 10.13   EUR/USD daily chart – long trade conclusion
Source: www.sharescope.co.uk. © ShareScope, reproduced with permission

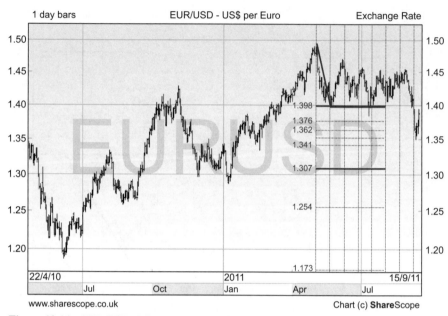

Figure 10.14   EUR/USD daily chart – short trade opportunity
Source: www.sharescope.co.uk. © ShareScope, reproduced with permission

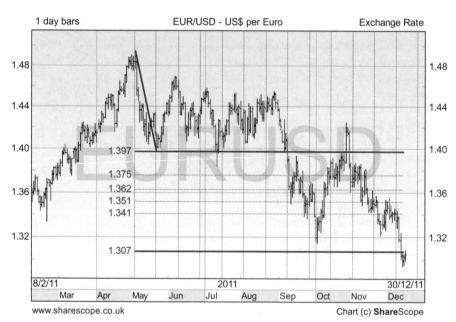

Figure 10.15   EUR/USD daily chart – short trade conclusion
Source: www.sharescope.co.uk. © ShareScope, reproduced with permission

CONCLUSION

It is good to remember that most indicators, used on their own, will only give you part of the full story. Also too many indicators can confuse you. So it's best to have no more than three indicators that complement each other.

Part IV
ENTREMET

These recipes for traders include some of my favourites. But because the frequency of how often they can be deployed is limited, but their accuracy is rather good, we love to use them, but only occasionally get the opportunity (certainly with New Issues, Turtle Soup and MAC-D). They bring you to the intermediate/advanced stage of understanding trading strategies.

> In the 14th century entremets began to involve not just eye-catching displays of amusing haute cuisine, but also more prominent and often highly symbolic forms of inedible entertainment.
> —Wikipedia

Recipe 11
MACD (Mac-D) and Friends
Difficulty Level: Intermediate/Advanced

In statistical terms, I figure I have traded about 2 million contracts ... with an average profit of $70 per contract. This average profit is approximately 700 standard deviations away from randomness, a departure that would occur by chance alone about as frequently as the spare parts in an automotive salvage lot might spontaneously assemble themselves into a McDonald's restaurant.

—Victor Niederhoffer

On Wednesday Niederhoffer told investors in three hedge funds he runs that their stakes had been 'wiped out' Monday by losses that culminated from three days of falling stock prices and big hits earlier this year in Thailand.

—David Henry (*USA Today*, 30 October 1997)

HISTORY OF THE RECIPE

MACD (pronounced 'Mac D') has been around for decades and attempts to depict likely future price movements. The stochastic and the relative strength index (RSI) are all variations on this theme. Just as a cookbook doesn't explain the DNA of an aubergine, but rather how to use it, so I will do the same with the indicators.

INGREDIENTS

The primary indicator is the MACD, which can highlight divergences, that is the price is making a divergence. For bullish momentum, the MACD is making higher lows (its low bases are rising) and the price is not doing the same. The idea is that the price too will start rising.

I use the MACD to confirm my view of a stock and I use the stochastic and RSI to support the MACD. You will need web charting or software charting.

RECIPE

Bullish signals

1. 'Bullish divergence': Here I am looking for the *MACD* to make a higher low and the price not to (see Figure 11.1 where price makes a lower low). I look to enter when the price eventually starts moving higher too.
2. I want the *stochastic* if possible to make a similar pattern (i.e. higher lows) but if it does not it is not necessarily a negative.
3. I want to see the *RSI* also make a series of higher lows, but it is not vital.
4. I tend to find if the *Bollinger bands* are close together then that can suggest a large price move is imminent.
5. I usually wait before buying for the price to move above the previous day's high or two-day high if I am being more cautious.
6. I always check the company news to ensure there is nothing negative and ideally that any recent comment from the company or about the company is positive.
7. I check my *Breadth radar* graph setting. Usually, I am not bullish if the *New Highs-Lows* is on a downward trend. Equally I am more short-term bullish if is it trending higher. I check the *Correlation* graph to ensure it is not too high (as a rough guide above 0.7 is high). Ideally, if I am going to beat the FTSE 100 or Dow, then there is little point picking stocks highly correlated to them.

When to sell and close the above position:

1. The *MACD* starts flattening out, moves horizontally and is in an overbought position.
2. The *stochastic* and *RSI* usually, but not always, start moving lower or making 'bearish divergences'.
3. The price makes a two-day low (one-day low if I am very risk averse).
4. I may close half my position and let half run if I am undecided.

Figure 11.1 shows the price, MACD, stochastic and RSI.

Bearish signals

1. 'Bearish divergence': Here I am looking for the *MACD* to make a lower high and the price to make a higher high. I look to enter when the price starts moving lower, perhaps a two-day low, preferably on some overall bad market or company news.
2. I want the *stochastic*, if possible, to make a similar pattern (i.e. lower highs) but if it does not it is not necessarily going to stop me making the trade.

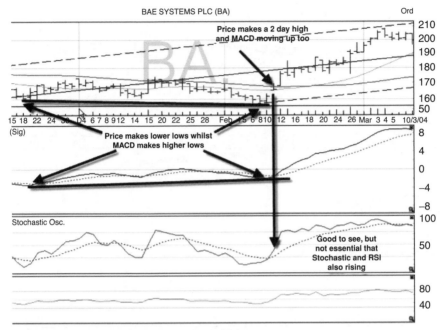

Figure 11.1 BAE Systems PLC – MACD bullish set up
Source: www.sharescope.co.uk. © ShareScope, reproduced with permission

3. I want to see the *RSI* also make a series of lower highs, but it is not vital.
4. I tend to find if the *Bollinger bands* are close together then that can confirm with the above signals that a large price move is imminent.

When to buy and close the above position

1. The *MACD* starts flattening out, moves horizontally and is in an oversold position.
2. The *stochastic* and *RSI* usually, but not always, start moving higher or making 'bullish divergences'.
3. The price makes a two-day high (one-day high if I am very risk averse).
4. I may close half my position and let half run if I am undecided as to whether the trend may continue.

Figure 11.2 shows the bearish set up.

THE INDICATORS

MACD (moving average convergence divergence) is an oscillator that is calculated by taking the difference between two exponential moving averages. A signal line

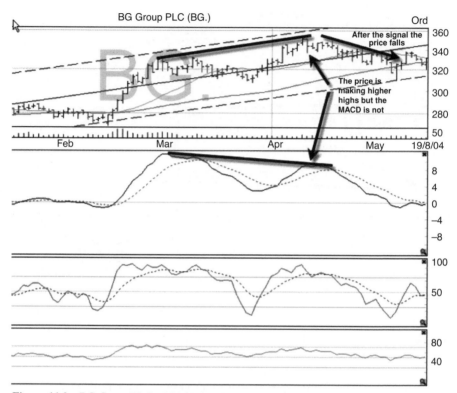

Figure 11.2 BG Group PLC – MACD bearish set up
Source: www.sharescope.co.uk. © ShareScope, reproduced with permission

is also plotted to help with interpretation. It is used to identify overbought and oversold conditions.

The *stochastic oscillator* is another indicator often used to identify when the market is overbought or oversold.

The *RSI* indicator measures a share's performance relative to its own recent price moves. It too can be used to gauge overbought and oversold conditions.

Bollinger bands are bands displayed on top of the share price. The width between the bands varies depending on the volatility of the share price. The greater the width the more volatile the share price; the narrower the width the less volatile the share price.

HERE'S ONE I MADE EARLIER

Figure 11.3 displays the chart for RIMM (Research in Motion), showing the price, the MACD, the stochastic and finally the RSI.

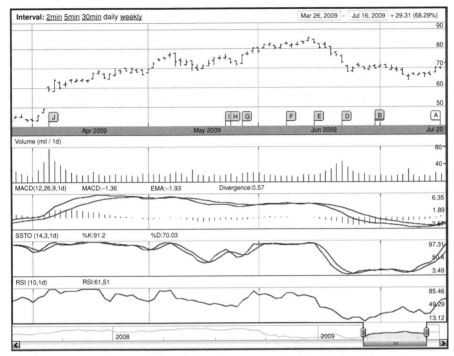

Figure 11.3 Bearish MACD signal in RIMM – long-term chart

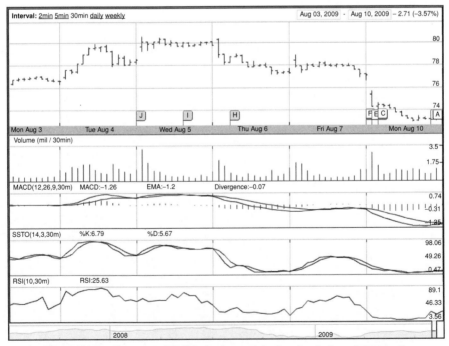

Figure 11.4 Short-term RIMM chart – used to pinpoint timing of short trade

The MACD shows the bearish divergence around mid-June 2009 with the price starting to decline. The stochastic tends to anticipate this a couple of days earlier and the RSI even before that.

The 30-minute interval bar chart illustrated in Figure 11.4 shows a divergence as Wednesday becomes Thursday.

Recipe 12
Nouvelle Cuisine: New Issues
Difficulty Level: Intermediate/Advanced

There's an expression I use in these instances: 'If you increase the price of an IPO, double my order – and if you cut it, cancel my order'.

—John Fitzgibbon

HISTORY OF THE RECIPE

Existing since the beginning of the stock market, this strategy, if executed correctly, can be better than mostly any others you will come across – we virtually built a hedge fund around it – but the private investor can assess it.

A new issue is a security that has been registered issued and is being sold on a market to the public for the first time. New issues are sometimes referred to as primary shares or new offerings. The term does not necessarily refer to newly issued stocks, although initial public offerings are the most commonly known new issues. Securities that can be newly issued include both debt and equity.

We are **ONLY** interested in equity.

INGREDIENTS

You will need access to all new issues coming out in the next three months. Also you need to know what has already come out in the last three months. A relationship with a broker would help also, as the distribution of most new issues will be through a broker.

This is more advanced as the premise is that you will have access to information that is not readily available until the listing. You need a relationship with a broker who has strong ties with leading brokers, i.e. those who actually help bring companies to the market.

RECIPE

Look for the following set up:

1. Know the offer price.
2. Has the stock based for more than four weeks, i.e. moved sideways in narrow range?
3. Know your financials, e.g. earnings per share (EPS), price earnings growth (PEG), management ability and so on.

Offer price: the price at which a broker is willing to sell a certain security for the first time.

Taking a leaf from Warren Buffett; when he first started, he was mostly concerned about the management and becoming a true owner of a company, not just a *shareholder.*

A longer period of static movement normally results in a greater breakout.

VARIATIONS TO THE RECIPE

Beware of false breakouts! See Figure 12.1.

Although this strategy is exceptionally good, there are times when the stock will do one thing then reverse and do the opposite – the old adage 'buy rumour, sell the fact' usually is to blame here. This is a market phenomenon where prices rise or fall on rumours and on the day of the actual factual statement, the security will reverse!

MORE ON THE RECIPE

Find more at:

http://www.newissuecentre.co.uk/index.htm for the UK
http://moneycentral.hoovers.com/global/msn/index.xhtml?pageid=10019 for the USA

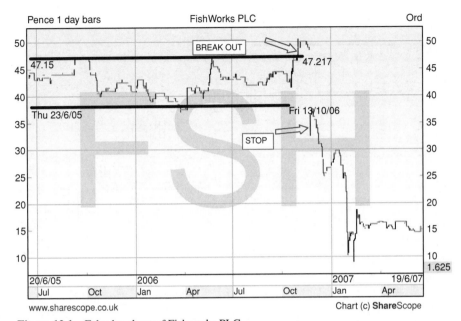

Figure 12.1   False breakout of Fishworks PLC
Source: www.sharescope.co.uk. © ShareScope, reproduced with permission

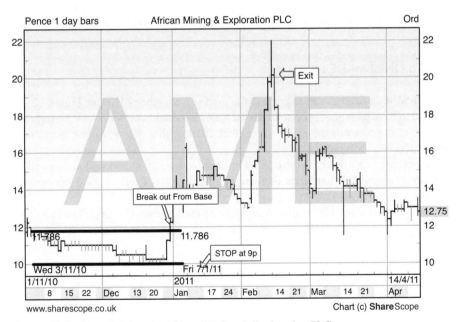

Figure 12.2   Long breakout in African Mining & Exploration PLC
Source: www.sharescope.co.uk. © ShareScope, reproduced with permission

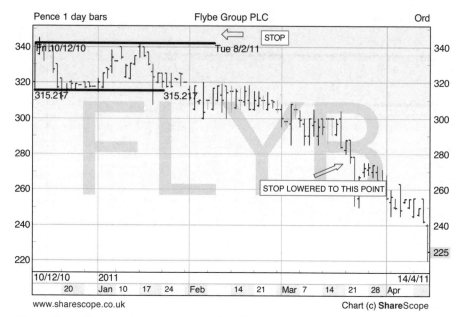

Figure 12.3   Short breakout in Flybe Group PLC
Source: www.sharescope.co.uk. © ShareScope, reproduced with permission

This strategy can be cooked up in any country with similar ingredients and tastes.

HERE'S ONE I MADE EARLIER

African Mining & Exploration came to the market November 2010 (see Figure 12.2). We had to have patience as the stock based for over a month, i.e. sideways movement. Bought at 13p towards the end of December 2010, with a stop at 9p, our target was above 30p. We took profit at 20p!

In December 2010, Flybe raised £66 million from a stock market flotation and is now listed on the London Stock Exchange (LSE: FLYB). This is a good example of a *short trade*.

The entry was at 312p and stop at 342p hence the risk was 30p. The stop has recently been moved to 280p making the risk: reward close to 1:1 (see Figure 12.3).

Recipe 13
Momentum: Short Termism Does Pay!
Difficulty Level: Intermediate/Advanced

I hope we can use the momentum from the weekend, but three days is a long time for softball.

—Deanna Gumpf

HISTORY OF THE RECIPE

Momentum breakouts occur around key support or resistance areas that have existed over multiple time frames. The most successful are the ones that occur with increased or better than average volumes and hence help create the real momentum. The momentum starts when the masses have recognised potential for profit. This also implies that once everyone is on the bandwagon there may be time constraints on how far the momentum will carry us.

INGREDIENTS

All you need is web charting or charting software which displays a clear histogram of the volume. Also desirable is the daily list of the most up or down stocks for the day. This will highlight the biggest movers that have largest volume.

RECIPE

Look for the set up shown in Figure 13.1.

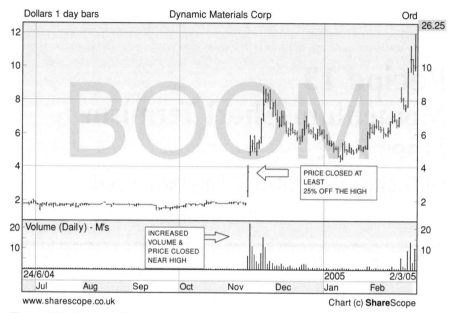

Figure 13.1   Dynamic Materials momentum trade set up
Source: www.sharescope.co.uk. © ShareScope, reproduced with permission

Notice how we could have played two strategies here: the *new issue* and *momentum*. This stock had been basing for much of 2004 before greater volume and interest took it higher. The gap and then the closing near the highs is a classic sign that this stock will continue the next day. Normally you need to look at stocks that have closed at least 20% or there about from their daily high on the day of the breakout. The volume is used to confirm that true interest is there.

If there is no gap, then this is still valid, as long as there is volume and it has 'broken out' from the base, or sideways, trading range.

VARIATIONS TO THE RECIPE

Of course the opposite holds true for going short. Also beware the *false breakout*, noting that the price closing near the high is the determining factor, even if the volume is there, as shown in Figure 13.2.

This is also known as a 'blow-off move'. These always need to be considered and hence these trades are best executed in the last 20 minutes of the market session. A blow-off move is when an increase in volume causes the price to move one way. From Figure 13.2, it can be seen that buyers become more prevalent during the session after a strong down move. This in turn causes the stock to reverse and you would go **long**

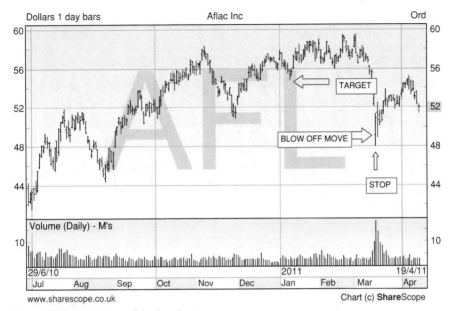

Figure 13.2 Aflac Inc – false breakout
Source: www.sharescope.co.uk. © ShareScope, reproduced with permission

as shown in the figure. Had the stock closed near the lows of the day, then we would have taken a short position. Again demonstrating why we wait until the end of the day to execute these types of trade.

These momentum trades can sometimes look perfect and due diligence has to be maintained, as even a perfect set up, i.e. stock that has closed right on its extreme and volume is there, may at first appear to be correct, but the next day you can still lose money. With momentum, expect volatility! You must place your target and be ready to get out at a moment's notice if you are wrong.

On the trade shown in Figure 13.3 we had our target at the most recent extreme low and were lucky. The alternative was to be stopped at a loss two days later.

> **Cooking Tip:** Momentum trades – expect to be out of the position the very next day, BUT if the stock continues then selling half and keeping half is a good idea to make the most of the continuation of possibly a new trend.

MORE ON THE RECIPE

Stop-losses can be very far away and this is one of the most risky strategies you will experience. Stops are normally placed below the breakout.

Figure 13.3   AGL Resources – 24-hour momentum trade
Source: www.sharescope.co.uk. © ShareScope, reproduced with permission

The trade ideas can be easily searched for through knowing what stocks have performed the best on any given day, a search you can do on Google or Yahoo! Finance for the most up or down for the day.

HERE'S ONE I MADE EARLIER

You will notice we are not looking to hold these positions for more than a week, unless the move follows through aggressively the next day. Risk reward could be as low as 1:1. We also do not always seek to see a *gap* in the market. We only want momentum. This is judged by the price move being greater than say 1.5 × ATR and the volume being greater than the daily average. Tata Motors Ltd, shown in Figure 13.4, is a classic example, of one that we had to hold for few days before we took profit.

Most momentum trades have some underlying reason for the move. The example in Figure 13.5 shows results for the stock of the Brown Group. Be aware of news about companies, the next day the press may publish more information and momentum could continue!

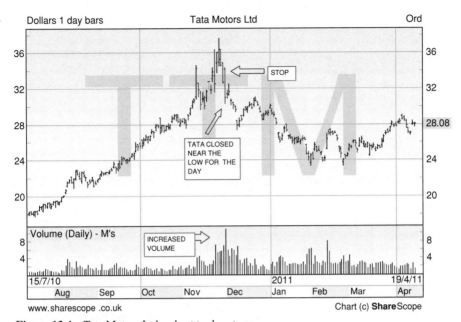

Figure 13.4 Tata Motors Ltd – short trade set-up
Source: www.sharescope.co.uk. © ShareScope, reproduced with permission

Figure 13.5 Brown Group – long trade set up
Source: www.sharescope.co.uk. © ShareScope, reproduced with permission

Recipe 14
Turtle Soup: The Most Famous Trading Recipe of All
Difficulty Level: Intermediate/Advanced

Behold the turtle. He makes progress only when he sticks his neck out.

—James Bryant Conant

HISTORY OF THE RECIPE

In the 1983 movie *Trading Places* starring Dan Aykroyd and Eddie Murphy, two wealthy investors have a bet to see if they can take a common criminal and make him into a successful trader.

In mid-1983 famous commodities trader Richard Dennis was having an ongoing dispute with his long-time friend Bill Eckhardt about whether great traders were born or made. Dennis believed that he could teach people to become great traders. Eckhardt thought genetics were the determining factor.

In order to settle the matter, Dennis suggested that they recruit and train some traders and give them actual accounts to trade to see which one of them was correct.

They took out a large ad advertising positions for trading apprentices in *Barron's*, the *Wall Street Journal* and the *New York Times*. The ad stated that after a brief training session, the trainees would be supplied with an account to trade.

This group was invited to Chicago and trained for two weeks at the end of December, 1983. They began trading small accounts at the beginning of January. After they proved themselves, Dennis funded most of the trainees with $1 million in February.

The students were called the 'Turtles.' (Mr Dennis, who says he had just returned from Asia when he started the program, explains that he described it to someone by saying, 'We are going to grow traders just like they grow turtles in Singapore.')

—Stanley W. Angrist, *Wall Street Journal*, 09/05/1989

The Turtles earned over $100 million over the next few years! A delicious recipe worth trying ourselves.

INGREDIENTS

- The rules on entry and exits and which markets to trade
- A calculator to calculate entry and exit levels unless you are good at mental arithmetic
- Web charting software

RECIPE

To understand the concept of basic set-up for this strategy we will use the chart for Microsoft Corp shown in Figure 14.1.

What to buy and sell

- We want to trade trendable markets and monitor enough markets to avoid getting no opportunities. We want to diversify to increase our chances of returns and that winning trades offset losing trades.

How much to buy or sell:

- This is based on the concept of N, which is the 'average true range' of the past 20 days. Most software packages will draw this so you don't have to. It is essentially a calculation of, on average, how widely the market tends to swing each day. We are trying to determine if there is a trend, or just general trading noise.

Figure 14.2 shows the average true range of the past 20 days on any given day. Zooming into the most recent date we can see precisely the price and the ATR.

- N also represents 1% of the account equity. For example, if you have $100,000 in your trading account then N is $1,000.

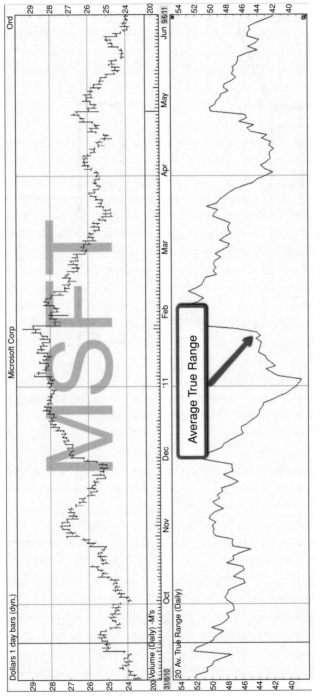

Figure 14.1 Microsoft Corp – ATR

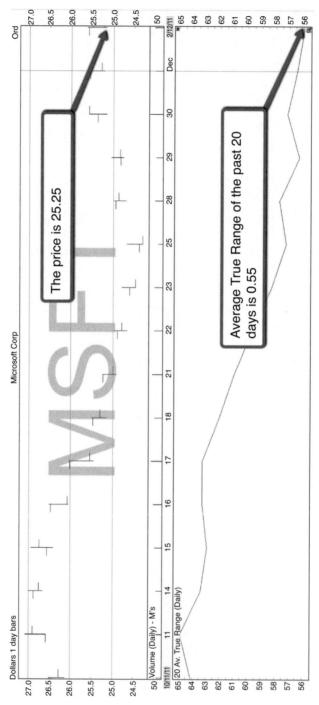

Figure 14.2 Average true range of the past 20 days

- So if N for GBPUSD is 0.0100 then you would want to ensure that on your account the most a 1N move resulted in was a $1,000 loss. So you would trade $10 per point (or the equivalent number of contracts – and that is called 1 unit) so a 100-point (N) move is $1,000.

Why this is such a delicious risk management recipe is that it achieves several things at the same time to give an outstanding flavour to your trading:

- Stops are based on N, they adjust therefore for the volatility of the market. They are wider stops for more volatile markets.
- However, there are few contracts for the more volatile markets so wider stops do not mean bigger losses.
- The equalised risk across markets means good diversification.

Entries

- Go long on a break above the 20-day high or short on a break below the 20-day high (Figure 14.3).
- Only initiate a trade if the last theoretical trade on this would have been a loss.
- If the last theoretical trade is a winner, then only enter when the price breaks out of the fail-safe breakout point of 55-day high (for longs) or 55-day low (for short).
- Add a second unit when the price has moved 1/2N in favour.

Stops and Exits

- Money management stops are placed at 2N away from the entry price of the last unit entered.
- Hence the risk for a 1-unit position is therefore 2N. For a 2-unit position the position risk is $3^1/_2$N (2N $+ 1^1/_2$ N). For a 3-unit position the total position risk is $4^1/_2$N (2N $+ 1^1/_2$N $+ 1$N). For a 4-unit position the total risk will be 5N (2N $+ 1^1/_2$N and 1N $+ ^1/_2$N). Since N also represents 1% of total account equity, the respective risks are 2%, $3^1/_2$%, $4^1/_2$% and 5%.
- Exits are a 10-day low (longs) and high (shorts).

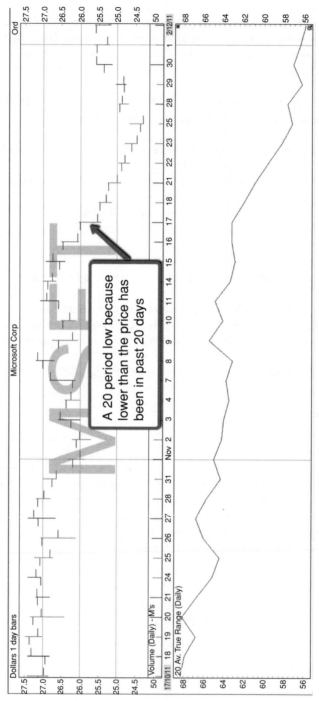

Figure 14.3 Microsoft Corporation short trade set up

Example

Crude oil
N = 1.20
55-day breakout = 28.30

	Entry price	Stop
First unit	28.30	25.90

	Entry price	Stop
First unit	28.30	26.50
Second unit	28.90	26.50

	Entry price	Stop
First unit	28.30	27.10
Second unit	28.90	27.10
Third unit	29.50	27.10

Other rules

- A single market should only have 4 units. In closely correlated markets 6 units and in loosely correlated markets 10 units and total limits are 12 long units + 12 short units. For example, 3 long positions of 4 units + 3 short positions of 4 units – which would be a total of 30% risk on the portfolio if all the positions turn wrong.

VARIATIONS TO THE RECIPE

The original turtles traded:

- 30 Year US Treasury Bond
- 10 Year US Treasury Note
- Coffee
- Cocoa
- Sugar
- Cotton
- Swiss Franc
- British Pound
- Euro
- Japanese Yen
- Canadian Dollar
- S&P Index
- 90 Day US Treasury Bill
- Gold
- Silver
- Copper
- Crude Oil
- Heating Oil
- Unleaded Gas

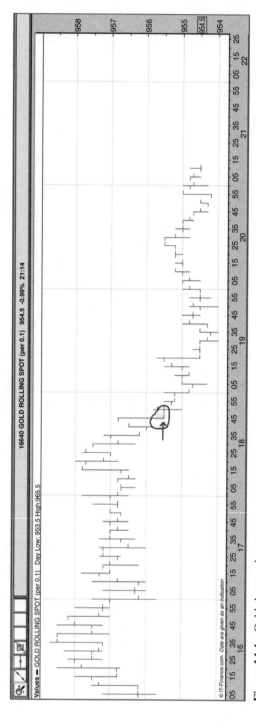

Figure 14.4 Gold short trade set up

Source: © Sterlingmarkets.com, reproduced with permission

MORE ON THE RECIPE

www.turtletrader.com describes in detail the background to not only this trading strategy but also many other trend-following strategies.

HERE'S ONE I MADE EARLIER

The 5-minute chart for Gold in Figure 14.4 shows the short entry where the price breaks below a 20-period low.

Recipe 15
Pairs Trading: One of Your Five a Day!
Difficulty Level: Intermediate/Advanced

Our mind is capable of passing beyond the dividing line we have drawn for it. Beyond the pairs of opposites of which the world consists, other, new insights begin.
—Hermann Hesse

HISTORY OF THE RECIPE

Pairs trading was pioneered by Gerry Bamberger and later led by Nunzio Tartaglia's quantitative group at Morgan Stanley in the 1980s. Pairs trading is a *market neutral* trading strategy enabling traders to profit from virtually any market conditions: uptrend, downtrend or sideways movement.

It is this term 'market neutral' that gave rise to this strategy. A market-neutral position may involve taking a 50% long, 50% short position in a particular industry, such as oil and gas, or in stocks from a particular peer group, for instance going long Ford Motor Company and going short Toyota, because you feel Ford may outperform Toyota.

For market neutrality to exist, then both the long and the short position must be of the same monetary value, e.g. you buy US$1 million of Ford and sell US$1 million of Toyota.

This is an advanced strategy because it is mainly executed by the larger hedge funds, which form a view on who will outperform or underperform across a peer group. This does not preclude individuals from taking advantage of such a strategy because technology allows us to both analyse pairs trading and execute it using our spread trading account or online futures broking account.

According to hedge fund research these strategies have yielded over 10% annual returns for hedge funds since 1990. And their volatility was only around 4%. That beats the FTSE and the S&P500 on return and on risk.

Cooking Tip: the basics of investing – Greater returns for lower risk.

Note, pairs trading is not a day-trading strategy; patience and proper analysis is needed.

INGREDIENTS

All you need is web charting or charting software which displays a clear list of all stocks in a relevant peer group or sector. You will need to ensure you know something about the fundamentals of the industry or how to evaluate stocks using fundamentals.

The following sites offer analysis for this type of trading:

www.pairstrade.com has a 14-day trial so you can test out the strategy.
www.pairtradefinder.com (used by hedge funds also) – A one-time fee applies of $497.

Once you know what you are looking for though you may not need to buy the software!

RECIPE

Look for the set up shown in Figure 15.1.

Notice that during 2008 to 2009 these two competitors seemed completely corre-lated. Indeed from about July 2008 Microsoft outperformed Apple, and a pairs trade selling Apple and buying Microsoft would have been the right trade. What we notice though, as the iPhone and awareness of Apple products and innovation grips the world from March 2009, you could have reversed the trade and go long Apple and short Microsoft.

The best execution is when both shares are very highly correlated, and the prices overlap each other as in April 2008 and again in April 2009. This means that any significant movement in one of the pair will trigger an almost exponential gain, usually around news items such as new product announcements.

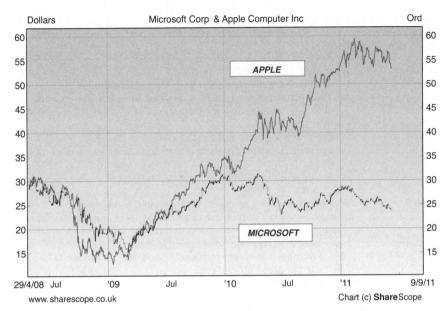

Figure 15.1   Trading example using US stock market giants Apple and Microsoft
Source: www.sharescope.co.uk. © ShareScope, reproduced with permission

---

Cooking Tip: Position size of the pair should be matched by dollar value rather than number of shares; this way a 5% move in one equals a 5% move in the other. As with all investments, there is a risk that the trades could move into the red, so it is important to determine optimised stop-loss points before implementing the pairs trade. Read more at www.investopedia.com/articles/trading/04/090804.asp#ixzz1P6Iu9mho

---

We have in monetary terms the same risk. What we are not completely certain of is exactly where our stop is. What we must do then is determine a monetary value on our stop. For instance, we need to control what we think is going to happen with what will actually happen. If Microsoft comes out with a far superior product, our long Apple in 2009 may not have been the right trade. Again professional traders will use a set figure, somewhere between 2% and 5% of the overall capital under management per trade risked. For instance, if my portfolio is $100,000 I will not want to lose more than $500 on this trade.

There are several methods of working out who will outperform and who will underperform. These include using:

• fundamental analysis on both

Table 15.1 Examples of news items

Type of news	Uses
Market news	Is the market in trouble?
	Is there much negative news that will stop stocks soaring?
	Are there economic problems? E.g. high inflation, low growth, strikes, political uncertainty, low productivity, all of which will impact stock price rises
Sector	Which sectors are rising and which falling?
	Is there sector rotation? I.e. some sectors are accelerating while others are falling
	Is there growth in certain sectors, e.g. technology; or trouble with others, e.g. consumer goods?
Industry	Which industries in a sector are going through good growth?
	Is there news about positive telecoms development or negative tobacco issues?
Company	Is the company generating sound positive stream of news?
	Or is it warning of earnings problems? Good news flows should be reflected in strong upward price moves. How is the price fairing?

- technical analysis on both
- specialist software

It is clear this is more of a fusion strategy between fundamental and technical analysis. Some of the news items to be aware of are listed in Table 15.1.

VARIATIONS TO THE RECIPE

Different strategies look at correlations between the market indices in general and those larger companies who have an international reach like Novartis (Swiss) and Pfizer (US) where you may have to consider the conversion in foreign exchange. We shall look at only one of these: the market index and the individual share. Note that many broking companies will allow you to trade in a single currency, like www.sterlingmarkets.com, a spread trading company, thereby allowing us to just get on and find good opportunities.

To find these opportunities we need to know a little about the beta of the stock. Beta is any number between −1 and 1. Zero implies that the stock will not be affected at all by the broader market; 1 implies it will move in tandem in the same direction and −1 is the exact opposite direction.

We can then use this information to find the extremes, stocks with a beta of either −1 or +1.

Once deciding upon a pairs trade where stocks are involved we will consider CFDs. CFDs are contracts for difference and one of the advantages of using these derivatives

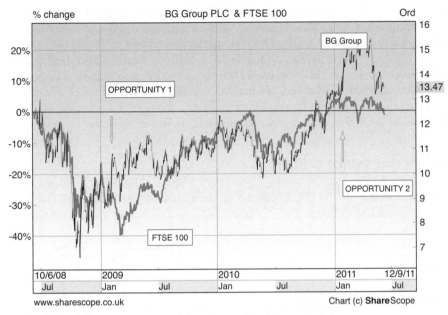

Figure 15.2   Pairs trading single stock CFD with the index that stock belongs to
Source: www.sharescope.co.uk. © ShareScope, reproduced with permission

of straight cash equities is that we do not incur stamp duty – keeping costs as low as possible.

We will look at the BG Group in the UK against the FTSE 100 index. BG has a beta of 0.89. We do not need to pick exactly a beta of 1, we simply need a divergence and if it is very close to 1 it will rarely diverge from the main index. I have included the chart in Figure 15.2 so you can see that in a period of three years only two real opportunities may have been obvious contenders for this strategy.

MORE ON THE RECIPE

While this type of intra-market strategy (i.e. CFD pairs trading) may be considered as lower risk than establishing a single CFD open position, this is mathematically misleading. Maintaining a spread position represents two open positions: one of which by definition is of a potentially unlimited contingent liability (the short sale). Therefore, the actual value at risk (VAR) is much greater than even the sum of the two parts.

Success is based on the trader's ability to spot anomalies in the market and to act quickly on them. These anomalies may persist for long periods and can disappear very quickly. It can take time to identify the price anomalies, as well as some discretion to determine when to enter and exit trades. These price anomalies do not occur very often, so it is important to have a solid plan to spot them and then to take the appropriate action when they do appear. Pairs trading results in double commissions being paid to the CFD provider since these trades involve two positions.

It is also important to have a stop-loss in place, even when trading pairs. Unforeseen events such as takeover bids, unexpected company announcements, profit downgrades and other market-related events can have an unexpected adverse impact on one leg of the pairs trade. A point of exit, either as a set percentage or a set dollar amount, needs to be determined before entering any trade, as mentioned before.

HERE'S ONE I MADE EARLIER

At the beginning of 2011, I noticed a strong correlation for Brent Oil and Crude Oil. As you can see from Figure 15.3, the prices were near each other and an opportunity

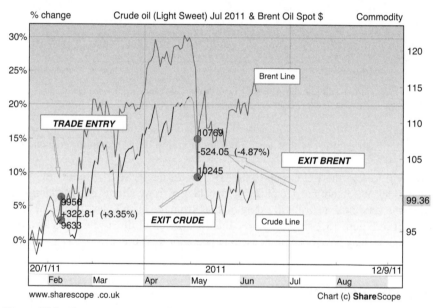

Figure 15.3 Same sector commodity pairs trade
Source: www.sharescope.co.uk. © ShareScope, reproduced with permission

Table 15.2 Entry and exits for Brent and Crude Oil

	Buy	Sell	P&L
Short Crude	10245	9633	−612
Long Brent	9956	10769	813
Total			201

arose in early February 2011 when the Middle East unrest caused a divergence. As with any human intervention there is an overreaction and in early May 2011 the position was closed – the entry and exits are shown in Table 15.2. The profit was 201 points overall and as the exact amount was put into both Brent and Crude, this equated to an actual profit of $4.87\% - 3.35\% = 1.52\%$.

Recipe 16
Double Big MAC-D
Difficulty Level: Intermediate/Advanced

Did you hear about that woman who got paid $3 million for spilling hot coffee on her crotch at McDonald's? Three million dollars!! I wish someone had given me that opportunity before I wasted all that time in college! If they had just laid it all out.

—Anon

HISTORY OF THE RECIPE

This strategy is based on the classical use of the MACD indicator but with slight twists that I think make huge improvements. As with all cooks the improvements come from experience.

INGREDIENTS

Web charting or software charting showing the MACD and stochastic indicators

RECIPE

Bearish signal to sell 'short'

1. First set up the daily price chart using the standard MACD default settings from the website or software package as shown in Figure 16.1. Repeat for the stochastic also indicated in Figure 16.1.
2. Check the stochastic is overbought, i.e. the main solid stochastic line is 80% or above.

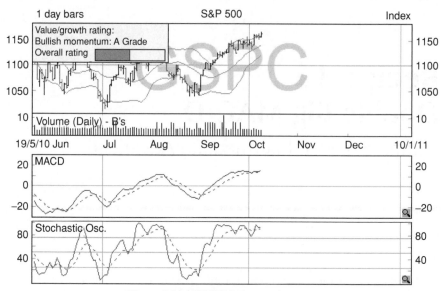

Figure 16.1   S&P500 short trade set up

3. Check the stochastic is showing a sell signal by falling below its dotted 'signal line'.
4. Check the MACD is moving sideways.
5. Check on the weekly price chart that the MACD is not rising sharply higher. If it is then you can proceed, but only with caution. Preferably the MACD has only just started moving sideways and on the weekly chart the stochastic is moving lower, either about to break through its own dotted signal line or already done so. If neither of these conditions is in place, we can proceed, but with extreme caution.
6. Sell 50% of your total desired position as soon as the price makes a two-period low, i.e. the lowest the price has been in two sessions. And sell the remaining 50% on a three-period low.

Figure 16.2 shows a weekly chart, i.e. each Open High Low Close (OHLC) bar represents one week. On it, the MACD is rising sharply. That means any moves down in the price are likely to be very short lived.

From Figure 16.3, at 9 August you can see that the MACD is moving flat. It is overbought, i.e. above 0. It is above its signal line (dotted line). The stochastic has not quite fallen through its dotted signal line on 9 August but is hovering just above it. If we work on the basis of 9 August that if the price falls below a two-day low then we will sell 50% of our position and sell another 50% on a three-period low.

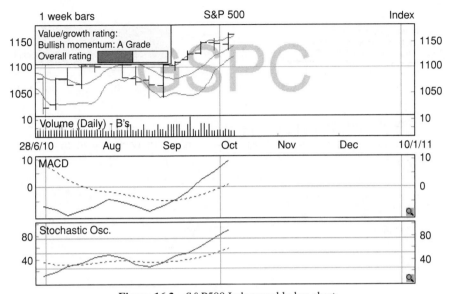

Figure 16.2 S&P500 Index weekly bar chart

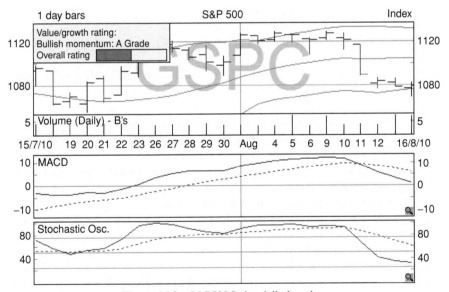

Figure 16.3 S&P500 Index daily bar chart

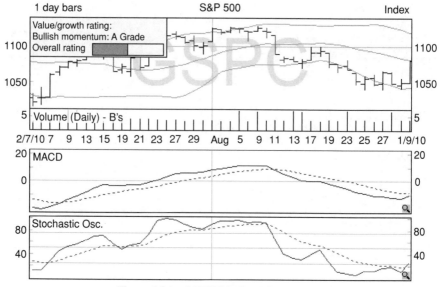

Figure 16.4   S&P500 Index daily bar chart

When to close the above position:

1. Option 1: if price makes a two-period high.
2. Option 2: if price makes a three-period high.
3. Option 3: if MACD on the daily chart is flat, then only if price makes a two-period high.
4. Option 4: if MACD is flat or rising on the weekly chart, then only if price makes a two-period high.

Option 1 is likely to get you out too soon, and then the price keeps falling. Whereas option 4 may get you out too late and you give away all your gains. There is no perfect recipe. It's a case of 'add to taste'. I usually go with option 4.

Figures 16.4 and 16.5 show the S&P500 over the same period. Figure 16.4 shows the daily price chart and Figure 16.5 shows the weekly price chart. Whether we look at the daily or weekly chart depends on the options above.

A different way of looking at this trading strategy is to treat signals in terms of confidence levels. See Table 16.1.

Yet another alternative is to say we are looking to sell short if the price falls to a two-period low. But we will only do this if on the daily chart our confidence levels are high. If they are low then we know we are taking greater risk and may not want to place the trade.

Figures 16.6 and 16.7 show the daily and weekly price charts for the same period for the S&P500, respectively. Look on the daily chart in Figure 16.6 on 13 May

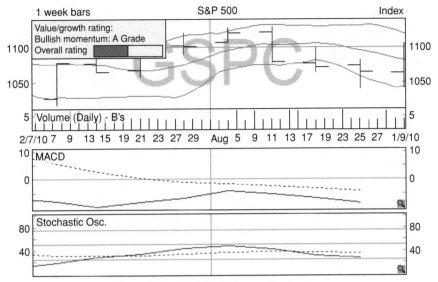

Figure 16.5   S&P500 Index weekly bar chart

(you'll have to count across from 10 May). Notice that the MACD is below 0 – i.e. clearly not a high confidence level. It is also already below the dotted signal line and is not a signal for us to sell. It is moving up (not sharply) – again, this is not a signal to sell. The stochastic is also moving up, overbought, i.e. above 0, and above its signal line. All conditions to say there is no reason to enter short.

However, after a period of market falls, as we see from 26 April, the market often has a bit of a move up, e.g. 8 May to 13 May. Most traders do not know if the moves are the resumption of an uptrend or a fake rally before a move down.

The way to know is to examine the weekly MACD. If it is falling, then you can read the daily chart thus:

1. Expect the MACD on the daily chart to be below 0; below its signal line, sometimes approaching its signal line. Similarly the stochastic will look as shown in Figure 16.6 on the daily chart. It looks like this because it has already been falling.

Table 16.1   Confidence levels

Sell short if:								
Daily (D) price or weekly (W)	MACD Flat	MACD Above signal line	MACD above '0'	MACD approaching signal line	Stochastic falling	Stochastic above '0'	Stochastic below signal line	Confidence level (High/Low)
D	Yes	Yes	Yes	Yes	Yes	Yes	Yes	High
W	Yes	Yes	Yes	Yes	Yes	Yes	Yes	High

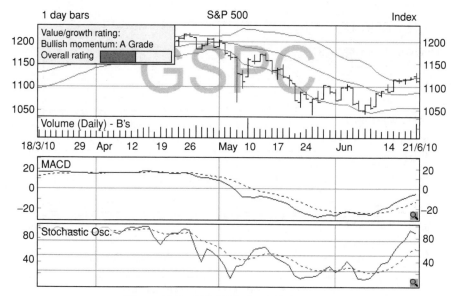

Figure 16.6   S&P500 Index daily bar chart

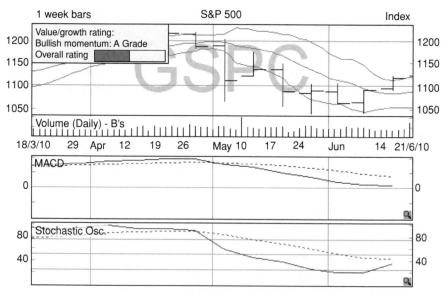

Figure 16.7   S&P500 Index weekly bar chart

2. Sell on a two-period price low.
3. If the weekly price chart MACD is rising and above its own signal line then do not sell short. If it is rising but below the signal line, and especially is approaching its signal line and is below '0', then that makes selling on a two-day price low on the daily price chart a lower risk trade.

For bullish signals

These are of course the reverse of the bearish signals.

HERE'S ONE I MADE EARLIER

Figures 16.8 and 16.9 show the daily and weekly S&P500 price charts over the same time period.

Let's look at 28 January. Notice that there has been a period of market declines. As is common the market then rallies. It rallies above a two-period high – on 1 February. But as you can see the market then continues to fall.

So if our 'buy' rule had simply been to buy on the price making a two-day high, we would have been wrong-footed. But we would not have bought, because as you saw earlier in this chapter, we don't buy if on the weekly price chart the MACD is below its signal line and falling sharply.

Now look at Figures 16.10 and 16.11, which show the daily and weekly charts for the same period for the S&P. Look at the long upward move lasting weeks. How do we ready ourselves for a potential short trade opportunity? Or indeed know if the party is over? If we start with the rule that a new two-day low is a good warning, then how do we know it will be the start of a new tradable downward move?

Well, we certainly won't do anything unless the weekly MACD is flat. And that only happens at the end of April. Moreover our confidence levels only start to rise when the daily MACD falls below its dotted signal line and that only happens clearly at the end of April.

Now look at 27 May in Figure 16.12. Why didn't we go long and buy then? After all it is a two-day high, the MACD is flat and the stochastic is rising. Well look at the weekly price chart in Figure 16.13 for the same period and security.

The weekly MACD is falling sharply. We would never go long unless it is at least flat on the weekly chart having fallen so sharply and is indeed below its dotted signal line, even if above 0.

Let's look at some variations on entry rules:

1. Buy to go long if stochastic rising
2. AND MACD is flat or rising
3. Ignore buy signal if weekly MACD is falling

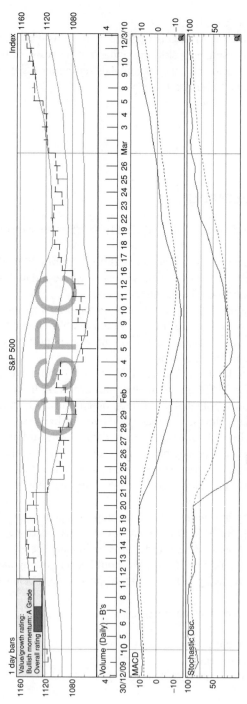

Figure 16.8 S&P500 Index daily bar chart

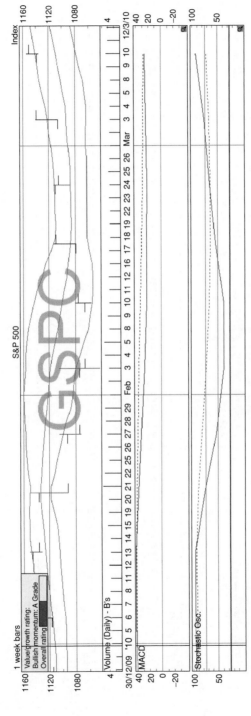

Figure 16.9 S&P500 Index weekly bar chart

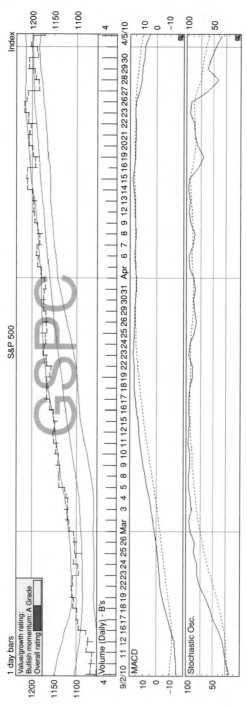

Figure 16.10 S&P500 Index daily bar chart

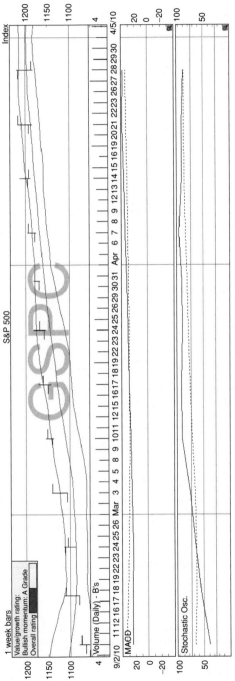

Figure 16.11 S&P500 Index weekly bar chart

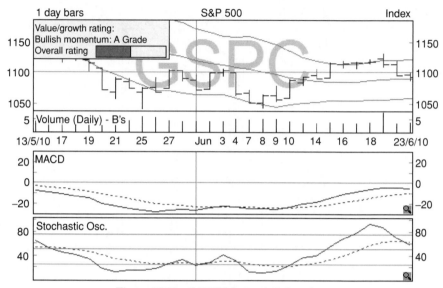

Figure 16.12   S&P500 Index daily bar chart

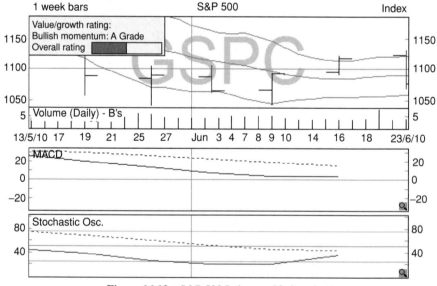

Figure 16.13   S&P 500 Index weekly bar chart

4. THEN buy on three-period high (i.e. highest price has been in last three periods (e.g. three days)

Let's look at some variations on exit rules for this difficult but well-worth tasting dish (assume we've bought a stock and are looking at when to exit):

1. Tight exit (i.e. risk-averse) trading options:
   a. Exit 100% of position if price makes a three-day low (i.e. lowest it has been for three days)
   b. Exit 50% of position if price makes a three-day low and sell the rest on a five-day low
   c. Exit 100% of position if the price makes a five-day low
2. Exit if:
   a. Stochastic overbought and falling
   b. AND MACD is at least sideways
3. Choose option 1(a) if weekly stochastic or MACD are sideways or rising and near but under their signal line – i.e. confidence is low of bullish momentum
4. Choose option 1(c) if weekly MACD is rising or sideways and above its signal line – i.e. confidence is high of bullish momentum
5. Choose option 1(b) in other situations to taste for risk

Part V
ENTREE

We now move to the advanced stage. Why? Well you should not be put off by these strategies and ought to know what many professional traders use. Whether you come to love them or not, it is important to understand all the trading games being played.

> It's not a huge deal. It's a logical, low-risk entrée into the equity underwriting business. The reality is that it is small for Chase, so if the bottom falls out, it's going to nick them only a couple of pennies.
>
> —Wikipedia

Recipe 17
English Breakfast or
All-Day Lunch
Difficulty Level: Advanced

Let me tell you something, Mister. If I had her money, I'd be richer than she is.
—Holly Golightly, *Breakfast at Tiffany's*

HISTORY OF THE RECIPE

The history of companies stretches back to Roman times, and deals principally with associations of people formed to run a business. A corporation is one kind of company, which means an entity that has separate legal personality from the people who carry out its activities or have rights to its property.

It was only in the mid-nineteenth century, the first being through the Joint Stock Companies Act 1856 in the United Kingdom, that private individuals could, through a simple registration procedure, be considered to have established a corporation with limited liability. Companies today dominate economic life in all developed countries and in the global economy. An important (but not universal) contemporary feature of a corporation is limited liability. If a corporation fails, shareholders normally only stand to lose their investment and employees will lose their jobs, but neither will be further liable for debts that remain owing to the corporation's creditors.

The institution most often referenced by the word 'corporation' is a publicly traded corporation, the shares of which are traded on a public stock exchange (e.g. the New York Stock Exchange or Nasdaq in the United States) where shares of stock of corporations are bought and sold by and to the general public.

The Exchange creates the market for the public. For there to be a market the participants must know what price a single share in the company is worth. This is why there is a now a law which demands that companies disclose their profits or losses along with a forward looking statement at least every six months.

INGREDIENTS

You need access to the internet as mostly all dates can be found through a simple web search.

Cooking Tip: You can also call your stockbroker for a list, that's what they are there for!

Also a charting package is required to make sure we can work out our risk/reward according to entry and possible exits.

We also need to ensure that the following is included in the mix:

- Price earnings growth (PEG) < 1.5 (an indicator which is a measure of how much a company is undervalued). It weighs the share price against how quickly earnings/profits are growing. Fast growing earnings in a company should reflect in a rising share price; if it does not, then the price may be 'cheap'. Usually a PEG under 1 suggests that the share price is not keeping up with the growth in earnings and so the stock is undervalued.
- Positive earnings over previous three years.

RECIPE

Look for companies that are in their *closed period*. This ensures that no news should come out from the company and the share price should travel north or south dependent on the previous statement of expectations. Look for an entry through trend following or breakout techniques and keep stops at 2N from entry where N is the ATR for the period. A closed period is about six weeks ahead of the actual results announcement date, so this gives a potential window of staying in the trade for the total length. Depending on the profit on the trade and if you have not been stopped out, take profits on the half or whole position the day before the results and remember to close no earlier than the end of business to take full advantage of the time value in the trade.

Figure 17.1 shows a classic example. Aberdeen Asset Management was reporting on 30 November, and we could have entered a *long position* early in August 2010 or waited for the closed period to begin and entered towards the end of October 2010. Once we know our ATR we can assume a 2N move against us will be our stop from the entry price. We MUST exit the trade a DAY BEFORE the results. We do not speculate the results are going to be good, bad or indifferent.

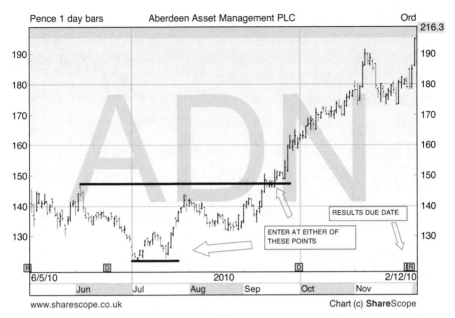

Figure 17.1 Pre-results trade Set up in Aberdeen Asset Management
Source: www.sharescope.co.uk. © ShareScope, reproduced with permission

After the results are announced, it is expected that all news about earnings and expectations should be available to the market. This is an *end of day trade* – with good volumes we buy or sell (in case of missing estimates) with a stop at an appropriate support/resistance level. These trades are momentum trades and are expected to carry 1% risk of overall capital invested. You would expect a write up in the press the next day and also over the weekend. Be wary when heavily tipped and use this as a potential exit signal.

At this point it is good to know again the PEG, earnings growth and the dividend policy. This, coupled with the Chairman's Statement and how the market responds, will give us an idea if we indeed wish to be holding this trade as an investment, i.e. our long lunch! See for example Figure 17.2.

From Figure 17.2:

1. Our first entry, during the closed period, we could have gone long at about 90p, with a stop below this point.
2. Our first exit as we do not have a crystal ball and do not actually know what will happen on 31 August 2010. So we make our 10% and get out.
3. We re-enter, the day of the results has sparked interest and this is shown by the increased volume, and the stock closing on its high. This would have resulted in a further 40% being added to our growth on this stock at least.

Figure 17.2   Post-results trade set up in Afren PLC
Source: www.sharescope.co.uk. © ShareScope, reproduced with permission

---

Cooking Tip: Do not fall in love with the stock. There are over 10,000 stocks in the USA and UK to pick from. It also means that if it is good to hold for several years then be prepared to do so. You need to know your fundamental analysis! Notice our risk does not change!

VARIATIONS TO THE RECIPE

The only lucrative variation is to follow the rules as set out by Warren Buffett or William O'Neill in investing for the ultra-long term. To give you an example of this it is best to consider William J. O'Neill's CANSLIM principle which you can read about in detail in his book, *How to Make Money in Stocks: A Winning System in Good Times or Bad*:

C – Current quarterly earnings per share have increased sharply from the same quarter's earnings reported in the prior year. (Beware of items in financial statements that can cause earnings distortions.)

A – Annual earnings increase over the last five years.

N – New products, management and other new events. In addition, the company's stock has reached new highs.

S – Small supply and large demand for a stock creates excess demand, and an environment in which stock prices can soar. Companies acquiring their own stock reduces market supply and can indicate their expectation of future profitability. Look for low debt-equity ratios.

L – Choose leaders over laggard stocks within the same industry. Use the relative strength index as a guide.

I – Pick stocks that have institutional sponsorship by a few institutions with recent above average performance. Be cautious of stocks that are over-owned by institutions.

M – Determine market direction by reviewing market averages daily.

MORE ON THE RECIPE

Table 17.1 provides a summary of this strategy.

Table 17.1   Pre-results strategy main points

Entry Strategy	Exit Strategy	Risk
Pre-results look to enter on first break in closed period. Post-results look to enter on the day of the results or on first pullback if the risk/reward is not at least 1:1. It could be that you enter when there is good volume and momentum exists, as long or short depending on the price closure in the top 25% of move for the day	Pre-results we exit a day before the announcement or where the price moves against us by 2N	Press has a lot of time to play with this over the weekend or the next day. The perception of brokers' comments could also move the stock adversely so quite high risk on the day – but pre-results should have consistent gains as no news is allowed out of the company and therefore limits your potential downside

HERE'S ONE I MADE EARLIER

Example 1

The best way to show the perfect set up is illustrated in Figure 17.3. Each trade will have its own quirks and this is an advanced study and will require much more analysis than would otherwise be required. Our example is related to Arm Holdings PLC.

1. Pre-result entry in closed period
2. First exit on profit which occurred a day before results
3. Day of results: 27 July 2010
4. Entry post-results on key support at 300p

Figure 17.3   Long trade in Arm Holdings PLC using pre-results strategy
Source: www.sharescope.co.uk. © ShareScope, reproduced with permission

5. Second exit pre-results on 1 February 2011
6. Day of results – no volume and so did nothing, the actual move was respectable though!
7. Post-results entered again with stop close to support of 500p

Example 2

Figure 17.4 illustrated our analysis for Atkins PLC.

1. Pre-result entry in closed period at 550.50p
2. Exit half the position at this point as momentum seems to have subsided. Keep stop for remainder of position at 500p
3. Day of results: 17 November 2011. Entry post-results at 560p on key support at 520p
4. With uncertain markets, we exited here at 640p

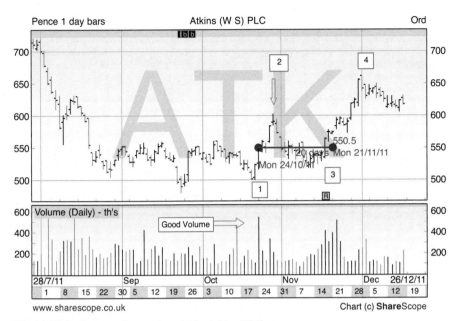

Figure 17.4   Long trade – pre-results in Atkins PLC
Source: www.sharescope.co.uk. © ShareScope, reproduced with permission

Recipe 18
Surfing the Waves: Fast Food
Difficulty Level: Advanced/Expert

I wouldn't be a brand new buyer of most companies...but old money should keep riding the wave. Don't get off the moving bus until it stops.

—Todd Campbell

HISTORY OF THE RECIPE

The Elliott wave principle is a form of technical analysis that traders use to analyse financial market cycles and forecast market trends by identifying extremes in investor psychology, highs and lows in prices, and other collective factors. Ralph Nelson Elliott (1871–1948), a professional accountant, discovered the underlying social principles and developed the analytical tools in the 1930s. He proposed that market prices unfold in specific patterns, which practitioners today call Elliott waves, or simply waves. Elliott published his theory of market behaviour in the book *The Wave Principle* in 1938, summarised it in a series of articles in *Financial World* magazine in 1939, and covered it most comprehensively in his final major work, *Nature's Laws: The Secret of the Universe*, in 1946.

INGREDIENTS

A charting package (available on all good platforms for trading) is sufficient. There are a limited number of charting packages that attempt to count the waves for you. I recommend you stick to manual counting as normally the human brain here will outperform the computer chip!

As you will soon discover the probabilities and combinations are so great that you may end up in a state leading to *analysis paralysis*.

We will only be looking at the set up that has the highest probability of being correctly labelled and hence tradable.

RECIPE

Just as McDonald's has found that fast food appeals to the masses, R. N. Elliott recognised a pattern that exhibits the behaviour of mass markets. There is only one reason for this! The laws of nature!

In an attempt to understand nature – patterns were derived. In nature they follow a sequence – the Fibonacci sequence. In markets this sequence has been used to varying degrees of success. What R. N. Elliott does is bring reasoning to the laws of nature that can be transposed to the markets – but not any market.

This only works in *very liquid* markets. The most liquid markets in the world are *foreign exchange markets*. So what is the set up we look for? Before we go into that we must become familiar with some very basic rules. We must also understand the *fractal nature* of this strategy.

Cooking Tip: Fractal implies that smaller time frame waves will exist and make up larger time frame waves. So when trading DO NOT MIX UP YOUR TIME FRAMES! This is best explained graphically. By counting the waves.

But first the RULES!

There are two basic types of wave: *impulsive* or *corrective*. These waves are described as the strong move in a currency's price coinciding with the main direction of the underlying trend. Impulsive waves are shown in Figure 18.1 as wave 1, wave 3 and wave 5. Corrective waves are shown in the figure as wave 2 and wave 4.

From this basic structure the rules are simple enough.

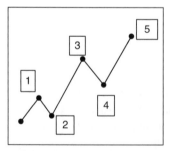

Figure 18.1 Impulsive and corrective waves

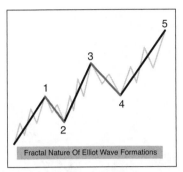

Figure 18.2   Fractal nature of Elliott wave formations
Source: www.rapidforex.com, reproduced with permission

A corrective Elliott wave 'count' must observe three rules:

1. Wave 2 always retraces less than 100% of wave 1
2. Wave 3 cannot be the shortest of the three impulsive waves, namely waves 1, 3 and 5
3. Wave 4 does not overlap with the price territory of wave 1, except in the rare case of a diagonal triangle

Figure 18.2 illustrates very clearly that each major wave is made of smaller waves and that internally within each wave the rules still apply. With this in mind we do not mix up our time frames, but use the smaller time frames to maybe pinpoint our entry. For instance if we know that impulsive waves are five in total and that correctives are three counter trend – we must try and count five waves up, three down and trade the next five up. We do not want to get into the complexities of all the different types of correctives and impulses. Remember: **KEEP IT SIMPLE!**

> **Cooking Tip:** To see the internal waves: drill down into smaller time frames. This allows you to decide best entry for a trade set up.

So look for the set up shown in Figure 18.3.

> **Cooking Tip:** Always pick the extreme high or low to begin your counting of waves!

1. Five waves up, this is your *first impulse*, and we know this because it is coming off a major low – in Figure 18.3 June 2010.
2. We know our corrective is complete, and we can label it **C,** when the wave following **C** enters into the price territory of the wave **A** – (recall the rules that

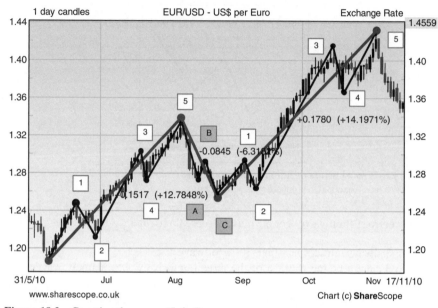

Figure 18.3 Counting the waves (5–3–5)
Source: www.sharescope.co.uk. © ShareScope, reproduced with permission

wave 4 cannot enter into the price territory of wave 1 – thus, this move cannot be an impulsive down).

3. Also note that the length of wave 1 (+12.78%) is the almost the same as wave 3 (+14.20%). Well we know that wave 3 cannot be the shortest.
4. This allows us to work out a phenomenally high risk/reward trade.
5. Our entry is above the 1.294 with a STOP below point **C**, as per rule 1 – wave 2 always retraces less than 100% of wave 1 as shown in Figure 18.4.
6. Mostly we are not concerned about wave 4 or wave 5 if we have taken our 'count' from an extreme high or low. They are important, but we want to make sure we only trade a certainty.

Cooking Tip: Once we know wave 1 has gone up by 12.78% as in Figure 18.3, then we should expect to make 12.78% as a bare minimum, as wave 3 cannot be the shortest.

VARIATIONS TO THE RECIPE

The art of counting waves is what makes all Ellioticians pour over endless charts and analyse endless impulsive and corrective waves. Figure 18.4 shows a daily chart and as you can see the opportunity to trade this set up did not arrive until September

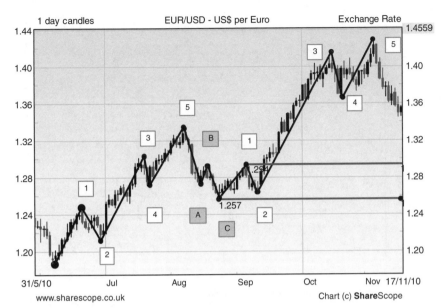

Figure 18.4 Finetuning our entry on EUR/USD
Source: www.sharescope.co.uk. © ShareScope, reproduced with permission

2010, nearly five months after the most recent extreme low was set. How then can we practically trade this set on shorter time frames? The short answer is you cannot be certain where you are in the wave count! But the rules do help us predict a change in direction. For this knowledge you need to know the make-up of corrective waves. We already know that impulsive waves are five waves up, and correctives are three down.

The extreme points are usually termed as *swing/pivot points*. Many strategies encourage swing trading because the most extreme high or low is a great place to put a stop should you be wrong. What Elliott wave theory explains is why these pivot points exist in the first place.

It is the drilling down into a smaller time frame that helps us understand the reason why we often hear of the term a *'V' shaped recovery*. See Figure 18.5.

Cooking Tip: Notice that the last wave of the impulsive and the first wave of the corrective are both made up internally of impulsives, i.e. wave 5 and wave A at the top Figure 18.5.

We will now use the above tip to help us trade shorter time frames with no regard for where we are in the wave count – we just want to look for five up and five down or five down and then five up! See Figure 18.6.

What we need to know is if before midday we had five waves up. If we did then we know this set up could be prime for a repeat of the move value of 12460 – 12395 =

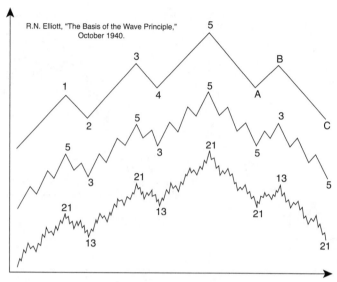

Figure 18.5 The make-up of v shapes

65 points. We enter on close of market and have a 20-point stop – hence looking to make 45. Risk/Reward = 20/45. For a day trade this is about right. We now move to say a 2-minute chart to ensure the wave before midday was indeed some kind of impulsive wave (see Figure 18.7).

The five-wave structure shown in Figure 18.7 is a type of impulsive wave called an *ending diagonal* (ED). We have our 5 up and 5 down, i.e. our 'V' shape indicating a change in trend. Normally an ED can be found at the top of a final move as predicted here, but this is probably not the place to explain the many different types of impulses and correctives. It is recommended, however, that you become familiar with the terminology and characteristics of waves.

As can be seen by the outcome (Figure 18.8) we counted correctly and we made our expected gain, i.e. the length of the price movement of our first wave down (as shown in Figure 18.6). The entry was 12452, and exit was exactly 40 points lower – the low was 12401.

MORE ON THE RECIPE

Characteristics of impulsive waves

Impulsive waves come in three main guises:

1. **Leading diagonal** – normally found at the end of a bear market
2. **Normal impulsive** – the generic five waves that make up the standard impulsive as shown in Figure 18.1
3. **Ending diagonal** – normally found at the end of a bull market

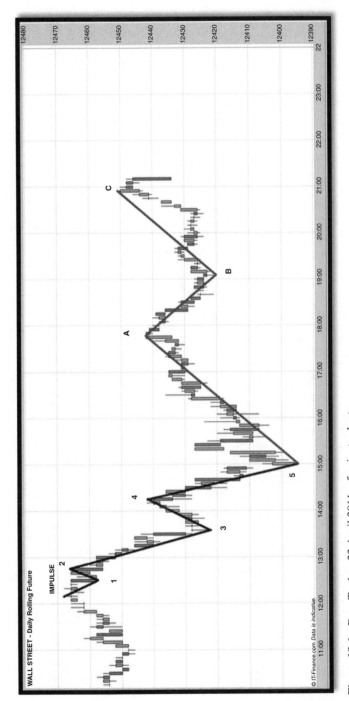

Figure 18.6 Dow Trade – 22 April 2011 – 5-minute chart
Source: © Sterlingmarkets.com, reproduced with permission

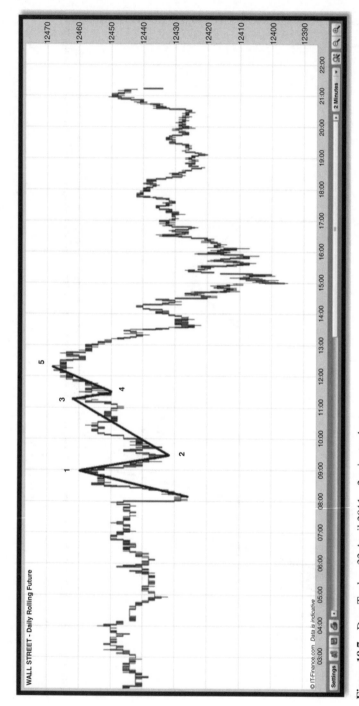

Figure 18.7 Dow Trade – 22 April 2011 – 2-minute chart
Source: © Sterlingmarkets.com, reproduced with permission

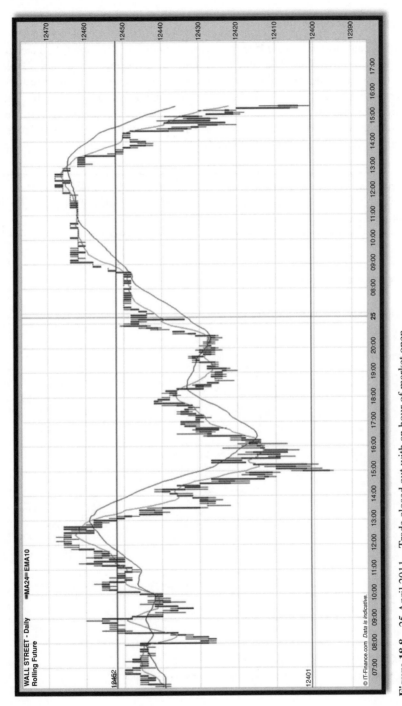

Figure 18.8 25 April 2011 – Trade closed out with an hour of market open

Source: © Sterlingmarkets.com, reproduced with permission

Characteristics of corrective waves

Correctives can form over 10 different wave structures and this is not the place to describe each in any detail. The general list consists of zigzags, triple and double zigzags, triangles (both expanding and contracting), flat patterns and double flats. The internal make-up of each can be very complex, and it is recommended that you seek to find only the basic 5–3–5 pattern where you trade the second five up or down.

Although currency is the best market to trade using Elliott waves, indices and some very liquid stocks follow the rules without fail.

> **Cooking Tip:** Always apply Elliott wave analysis to LIQUID MARKETS. They perform the best with herd mentality and hence follow the rules of nature better than illiquid markets!

HERE'S ONE I MADE EARLIER

Figure 18.9 charts the daily S&P trade.

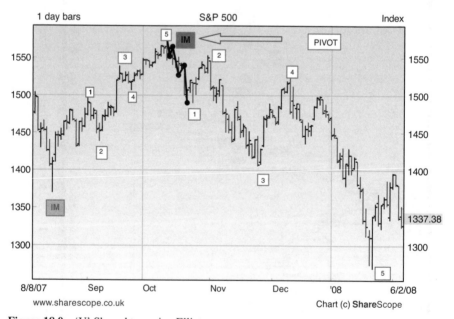

Figure 18.9 'V' Shaped top using Elliot waves
Source: www.sharescope.co.uk. © ShareScope, reproduced with permission

Again this was one to wait out! This was October 2007 and after looking for a five-wave up then a five-wave down we entered a short close to the top of this market. These opportunities do not arrive very often but helped us achieve a 248% return for the year 2007/2008. The five waves down was our clue.

Not for the faint hearted this requires many years of understanding the intricacies of each wave and its component parts. It is best to stick to the most obvious 5–5–3–5 set up, and look to trade the final five waves. ONLY for the intermediate skilled!

Part VI
MAIN

These are for the Cordon Bleu trader. They may appear esoteric but if, like so many traders, you move from simply equities and forex to the potentially lucrative world of options and bonds then you will need to be armed with these techniques.

> For many of these young broadband users, the Internet is their main course for news, and they don't always eat their vegetables or order dessert in the form of using other media.
> —John Horrigan

Recipe 19
Coffee Options and Spreads
Difficulty Level: Advanced/Expert

Money is one of the last things we worry about and people shouldn't get hung up on the numbers, except to realize that it gives us options.

—Christopher Blizzard

HISTORY OF THE RECIPE

Contrary to popular belief, options trading, or the use of options as a financial instrument, isn't a new innovation at all. In fact options trading has a much longer history than most people realise; a history that goes way back to the times before Christ was born. Indeed, options trading has come a long way to become the most versatile trading instrument in the world today. Options trading did not just spring from the drawing boards of some financial scientist. It has evolved over thousands of years and understanding the history of options trading gives options traders an appreciation of the depth of this renowned trading instrument.

Option Basics

Definition: An option contract is an agreement between two parties to buy/sell an asset (e.g. stock or futures contract) at a fixed price and fixed date in the future.

It is called an option because the buyer is *not obliged to carry out the transaction*. If, over the life of the contract, the asset value decreases, the buyer can simply elect not to exercise his/her right to buy/sell the asset.

It is surprising that there is confusion surrounding options considering there are only two types:

1. **CALL OPTION** – gives the holder the right to buy an asset at a certain price within a specific period of time.
2. **PUT OPTION** – gives the holder the right to sell an asset at a certain price within a specific period of time.

Let us look at both types of options in a bit more detail.
You will need to know the following terms:

- **Strike price** – price at which an underlying stock can be purchased or sold.
- **Time value** – time remaining until expiration.
- **Premium** – the deposit paid to secure the option to buy or sell at the strike. An option's premium is its intrinsic value + time value.
- **Breakeven** – strike price + premium paid.
- **ATM (at the money)** – where strike price of option is at or close to actual market price.

It can get quite complicated to find the premium price and the explanation is outside the extent of this book. We just need to know how best to trade and make profits regardless of the terminologies detail. For example you do not need to know the inner workings of a car to drive it, but you do need to know how to turn it on, where the brakes and accelerator are and general road traffic rules to be competent. So back to basics! The best way to describe the inner workings is by looking at the risk charts for each type of option.

Nothing helps an option trader understand the risk/reward characteristics of an options trading strategy or stock options position better than *risk graphs*. Risk graphs are visual tools, taking the form of a chart, presenting the behaviour of an option position across a spectrum of stock prices at expiration or at a specific number of days before expiration. Risk graphs allow options traders to instantly evaluate if the risk/reward characteristics of an options trading strategy suit the intended investment objective before actually executing it. Risk graphs pinpoint at a glance where the areas of highest gains and losses are, allowing options traders to make more educated decisions without complex calculations.

Call Option

A call option is simpler to describe in graphical form. The main points to note:

- Bullish strategy, in that the prices of the underlying stock or futures are expected to rise (Figure 19.1).
- Bearish strategy (*sell call*), the expectation is that you will keep a premium if underlying stock or futures go below the strike price (Figure 19.2).

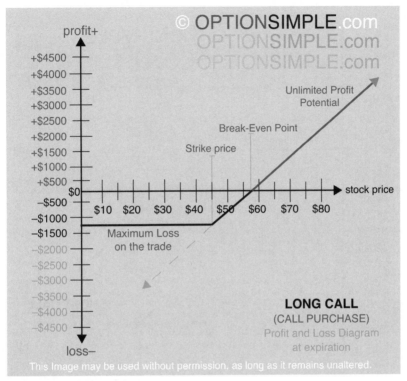

Figure 19.1   Call option: bullish strategy
Source: © Optionsimple.com

Someone who has taken the opposite side of a long call/put is said to be short the call/put.

Put Option

- **Long put – bearish strategy,** the expectation is that prices will fall in underlying stock or futures, and the maximum profit is gained if the underlying stock or futures go to zero (Figure 19.3).
- **Short put – bullish strategy**, the expectation is that prices will rise and the seller keeps the premium (Figure 19.4). Risk is unlimited.

I do not believe you need to know much more than this for what we are about to show you. There are some very complicated strategies, but if our aim is to simply make money with adequate and better than average risk control then we can and should be able to add hard cash to our bank accounts.

The following concerns the details about the spreads we want to use, which both limit our risk and help us to maintain a constant income. We will only be looking for a

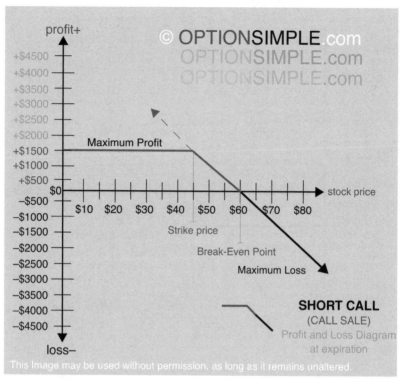

Figure 19.2   Call option: bearish strategy
Source: © Optionsimple.com

particular type of trade and will not be looking at the plethora of strategies available. Knowledge of options terminology and jargon will be kept to a minimum, but we cannot escape it unfortunately!

You can see from the above options risk graphs that you could have unlimited risk if you take the other side of the purchase of a call or put. There is always more risk in writing options, i.e. selling options.

Credit Spreads

Investment Objective – CREDIT

The clue is in the title. We will be using a combination of calls or puts to create a spread trade that delivers a credit to your trading account. We will not complicate the strategy and we will consider two types:

- PUT BULL SPREADS – use only puts with the same expiration.
- CALL BEAR SPREADS – use only calls with the same expiration.

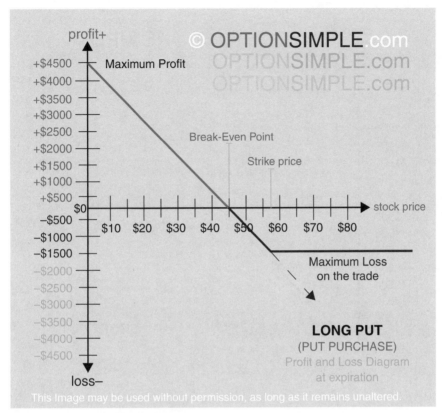

Figure 19.3   Put option: bearish strategy
Source: © Optionsimple.com

Option Chain

This is the list of prices (premiums) for both calls and puts for a specific stock and we will use Apple Inc. as an example as shown in Figure 19.5. We will need to understand how to read the chain.

Note that in Figure 19.5 the calls are on the right and the puts are on the left. The middle section contains the strike prices. We now have all we need to begin!

Put Bull Spreads

How to make a put bull spread:

1. Purchase a single *at the money* put contract.
2. Sell a single *in the money* put contract.

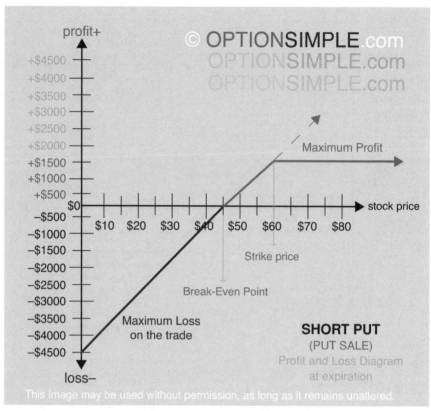

Figure 19.4 Put option: bullish strategy
Source: © Optionsimple.com

The current quote for Apple is shown above the chain. *Last* is the last price traded: currently –$349.71. You will very rarely, if ever, be able to get a strike price which is absolutely at the money. So let's make our spread!

1. BUY JUL 11 350 PUT @ $15.45
2. SELL JUL 11 370 PUT @ $27.00

Cooking Tip: It may seem obvious but to create a credit we have to sell and hence receive more than we pay out. You want to pick a chain about 40–60 days from the trade date.

Credit is simply $27.00 – $15.45 = $11.55

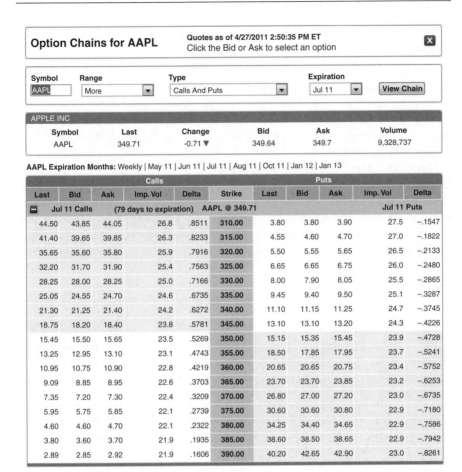

Figure 19.5 Option chain
Source: www.optionsxpress.com

Strategy

Wait for the price to move above the short put strike price. Pick strikes that will provide the credit. Let both puts expire worthless.

Maximum risk = Difference between long and short put strike prices – Initial credit
Loss = Short put strike price – Long put strike price – Initial credit

The reward of a put bull spread is limited to the initial credit made when entering the trade. The profit of a put bull spread is calculated as:

Maximum profit = Initial credit
Profit = Short put premium – Long put premium

Remember one option contains 100 shares and so $11.55 credit is $1,155 actual credit.

INGREDIENTS

Knowledge of the terms 'in the money' (ITM), 'out the money' (OTM), and 'at the money' (ATM) is an absolute necessity for this strategy. What will help us is if we already hold shares.

This strategy is not so simple that you do not need a charting package to determine the general direction of a stock or future. We may also have a view of the fundamental value of a stock. Either way we need to know if the stock is going up, down or sideways. For this to hold true we use options as a vehicle to limit our risk and maximise our profits from simple charting techniques already discussed in other parts of this book.

RECIPE

The steps are easy enough:

1. Pick a stock or market liquid enough for there to be options associated with it.
2. Decide if the chances of a sideways market will occur using technical analysis.
3. Configure the credit spread on whether the market is bullish or bearish.

Cooking Tip: Be aware that American style options rules are different from European. With American style options you can be exercised on your short option at any time – not just at expiry.

VARIATIONS TO THE RECIPE

Call Bear Spreads

How to make a call bear spread:

1. Purchase a single *higher strike call* contract.
2. Sell a single *lower strike call* contract.

The characteristics are:

- Limited risk: the most you can lose is the difference between strike prices and the credit
- Limited reward: the credit received from placing this trade
- Breakeven = Lower strike + Net credit received

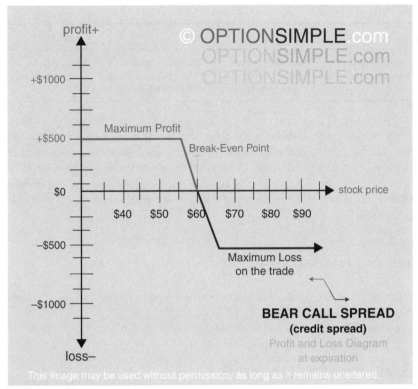

Figure 19.6   Bear call spread
Source: © Optionsimple.com

See Figure 19.6 which illustrates a risk graph for this type of spread.

MORE ON THE RECIPE

The Greeks

Options pricing is an involved science and for more complicated strategies you must get to know your Greeks – no, not the language, but the predefined elements of any pricing model. They give you a slight spin on what may actually be going on in the underlying market.

The Greeks help to provide important measurements of an options position's risks and potential rewards. Once you have a clear understanding of the basics, you can begin to apply this to your current strategies. It is not enough to just know the total capital at risk in an options position. To understand the probability of a trade making money, it is essential to be able to determine a variety of risk-exposure measurements.

Table 19.1   The Greeks

Vega	Theta	Delta	Gamma
Measures impact of a change in volatility	Measures impact of a change in time remaining	Measures impact of a change in the price of the underlying	Measures the rate of change of delta

Since conditions are constantly changing, the Greeks provide traders with a means of determining how sensitive a specific trade is to price fluctuations, volatility fluctuations and the passage of time. Combining an understanding of the Greeks with the powerful insights the risk graphs provide can help take your options trading to another level. The Greeks are displayed in Table 19.1 with a short description of why they are used.

HERE'S ONE I MADE EARLIER

The current quote for Apple is shown above the chain in Figure 19.7. *Last* is the last price traded: currently –$349.71.

The trade we did was the credit spread – call bear spread.

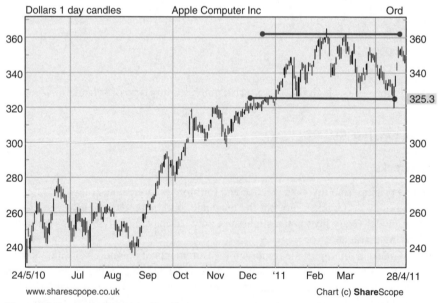

Figure 19.7   Apple Computer Inc chart
Source: www.sharescope.co.uk. © ShareScope, reproduced with permission

					Calls					
▲Strike▼	Last	Chg	Bid	Ask	Day High	Day Low	Vol	Opint	Action	
Weekly							expires 7/1/2011			
290.00	36.15	0	36.35	36.55	0	0	00	11	Detail	
295.00	0	0	31.40	31.65	0	0	00	0	Detail	
300.00	26.20	0	26.45	26.70	0	0	00	23	Detail	
305.00	21.70	0	21.60	21.90	0	0	00	60	Detail	
310.00	16.90	0	16.85	17.15	0	0	00	75	Detail	
315.00	12.44	0	12.40	12.65	0	0	00	91	Detail	
320.00	8.30	0	8.30	8.65	0	0	00	430	Detail	
325.00	5.15	0	5.05	5.30	0	0	00	911	Detail	
330.00	2.80	0	2.70	2.82	0	0	00	2,565	Detail	
335.00	1.25	0	1.20	1.34	0	0	00	10,294	Detail	
340.00	0.59	0	0.57	0.62	0	0	00	9,652	Detail	
345.00	0.24	0	0.24	0.29	0	0	00	327	Detail	
350.00	0.12	0	0.10	0.16	0	0	00	168	Detail	
355.00	0.08	0	0.03	0.14	0	0	00	10	Detail	
360.00	0.05	0	0.04	0.10	0	0	00	4	Detail	
365.00	0	0	0	0.08	0	0	00	0	Detail	
July 2011							(19 days to expiration)			
290.00	36.80	0	36.90	37.20	0	0	00	2,114	Detail	
295.00	31.65	0	32.20	32.45	0	0	00	1,288	Detail	
300.00	27.60	0	27.60	27.85	0	0	00	7,115	Detail	

Collapse All · Disable Roll Overs

Figure 19.8 Option prices for different strike levels

First we look at Apple stock on the chart and take a view. You can see from the chart that the price seems to have approached the top of a range and could be coming lower to stay in the range. So we look for a credit spread that makes us money if the stock falls.

Our spread from the chain will be:

1. Purchase a single *higher strike call* contract.
2. Sell a single *lower strike call* contract.

This will give us:

1. BUY JUL 11 355 CALL @ $13.10
2. SELL JUL 11 335 CALL @ $24.55

Our Credit = $24.55 − $13.10 = $11.45, as we did a single option the credit is 100 (number of shares in option) × $11.45 = $1,145.

Several weeks later and this same chain stands as Figure 19.8. Note the date 26 June 2011. Trade was executed on 27 April 2011. This trade was closed on Friday 24 June 2011, and the option chain shows us where we stand.

To close the trade we did the opposite

1. SELL JUL 11 355 CALL @ $0.03
2. BUY JUL 11 335 CALL @ $1.34

Our total cost here is −$1.34 − $0.03 = $1.31, so total debit = 100 × $1.31 = $131
Our total profit = $1,145 − $131 = $1,014

Recipe 20
Bonds: Shaken Not Stirred
Difficulty Level: Advanced

> After the market sells off, like you saw [Thursday], you want to see the bond market rising, because what it tells you is that money is not leaving the financial system.
>
> —Ronald Hill

HISTORY OF THE RECIPE

Feudal times in thirteenth-century Europe set the scene for the beginning of the bond market. The Italian peninsula was controlled by the states of Tuscany, Venice and Florence, each classed as kingdoms in their own right. These independent kingdoms tended to have regular feuds about trade, which would often lead to wars.

These wars had to be paid for and, to give the local army an impetus, mercenaries were hired – who were never cheap. So the states offered bonds to the very wealthy citizens to raise funds that were used to pay the mercenaries – if the bonds stopped so did the wars. There is no need to go into the circumstances or the reasons too much, but do understand that the existence of bonds has a very sinister beginning.

Back to modern times and if a government wants to raise money without increasing taxes or disposing of assets, it sells bonds to investors. Bonds are a promise to pay interest, usually a fixed amount at set intervals, and to return the investor's capital on a specified date.

Bonds are popular with many investors, particularly banks, insurance companies and pension funds, largely because their returns are certain (assuming that the borrower doesn't decide to renege on its debts).

A bond's market price, like the price of any financial asset, represents the *present value* of the stream of future cash flows to the bondholder. The price of a bond is a function of the coupon of the bond relative to the market yield of equivalent bonds.

For example, a bond with a coupon rate of 5% will be priced at par if the market yield is also 5%; if the market yield is below 5%, the bond will trade at a *premium*; and if the market yield is above 5% the bond will trade at a *discount*. Since bond prices fluctuate with changes in market yields or the general level of interest rates, in order to determine the factors that influence bond prices we need to understand what factors influence the general level of interest rates.

INGREDIENTS

There are limited reliable resources to help private investors compare current prices of bonds.

The Securities Industry and Financial Markets Association (SIFMA) is a leading securities industry trade group representing securities firms, banks and asset management companies in the United States and Hong Kong. SIFMA was formed on 1 November 2006, and offers investor education web sites, such as www.investinginbonds.com and www.investinginbondseurope.org, showing recent and historical price data on corporate and municipal bonds. Investors can sort and search the data by a variety of criteria and broad categories, such as yields, ratings or prices.

The European High Yield Association (EHYA) in London is a trade association representing participants in the European high yield market. Members include banks, investors, issuers, law firms, accounting firms, financial sponsors and others in the European high yield market.

The key to everything is to simplify it – especially when the understanding of a new concept may not be so clear.

Cooking Tip: a bond is an IOU, and so long as IOU, I will pay you interest, until I pay back my loan. The interest is sometimes referred to as a coupon and the IOU is the principal amount. These IOUs come in various shapes and sizes.

It is important to understand that the yield or coupon on bonds is the most important singular item when it comes to trading these instruments.

A term you should become familiar with is the *yield curve*, which is a graph of the yields of closely related bonds of different maturities. The vertical axis of the graph represents the yield, and the horizontal axis represents the time to maturity.

There are four basic types of yield curve:

1. The upward sloping curve is historically the norm given the normal relationship that the longer the time to maturity, the higher the yield. This is shown in Figure 20.1.

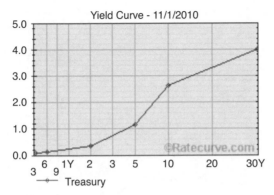

Figure 20.1   An example of the yield curve
Source: © ratecurve.com, reproduced with permission

2. An inverted yield curve occurs when interest rates are very high and expected to fall.
3. A flat yield curve indicates that the term to maturity has no impact on interest rates.
4. A humped yield curve initially rises, but then falls for longer maturities. Inverted and flat yield curves are fairly rare. In recent years institutional investors have had high demand for the 30-year long bond, which has raised its price to the point that it often yields less than the 20-year long bond. This has caused the humped curve to be the most common shape in recent years.

The shape of the yield curve changes with the business cycle and has been a good leading indicator of economic activity. A steeply positive sloped yield curve is indicative of an economic recovery, and is often found at the end of recessions. Its shape reflects market expectations of a significant increase in interest rates and the fact that the US Federal Reserve Bank ('Fed') is keeping short-term rates low to aid a slumping economy recover.

Inverted curves often precede an economic downturn. A flat yield curve is often the result of the Fed raising short-term rates to cool an overheated economy. Flat yield curves are rare and do not last very long when they appear.

Many bond traders use the shape of the yield curve to derive trading strategies. As of June 2011 the US bond market yield curve looked as shown in Figure 20.2.

RECIPE

Bonds can be issued by either governments or corporates. The ultimate risk is of default and corporates are considered more risky simply because of the fact that governments rarely default. In recent times this has been subject of speculation when

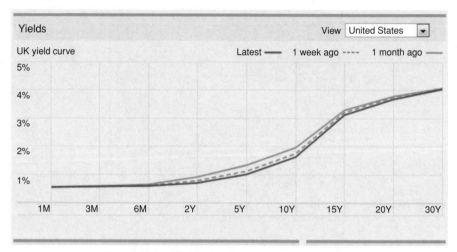

Figure 20.2 US bond market yield curve, June 2011

you consider Greece, Portugal and Ireland. So what do we put into this recipe and what is the best set up? Remember keep it simple.

Strategies for bond investing range from a buy-and-hold approach to complex tactical trades involving views on inflation and interest rates. As with any kind of investment, the right strategy for you will depend on your goals, your time frame and your appetite for risk.

The factors below help determine the value of your bond investment and the degree to which it matches your financial objectives:

- credit quality
- credit rating
- bond insurance – financial guaranty insurance
- price
- yield
- market fluctuations – the link between price and yield
- interest rates – inflation, central banks and inter-bank rates
- tax or fiscal status
- assessing risk
- link between interest rates and maturity
- bond's maturity
- redemption features

The most common trade by professionals is trading the yield curve!

Changes in the shape of the yield curve will change the relative price of bonds represented by the curve. For example, suppose you have a steeply upward sloping yield curve like the one shown in Figure 20.2.

Let's say on this curve the 2-year bond is yielding 0.94% and the 30-year bond is yielding 4.50% – a spread of 3.56%. This may lead a trader to feel that the 30-year was cheap, relative to the 2-year. If that trader expected the yield curve would flatten, he could simultaneously go long (buy) the 30-year and sell short the 2-year. Why would the trader execute two simultaneous trades rather than simply buying the 30-year or selling short the 2-year? Because if the yield curve flattens, reducing the spread between the 2-year and the 30-year, it could be the result of the price of the 2-year falling (increasing the yield), or the price of the 30-year increasing (decreasing the yield), or a combination of the two. For the trader to profit from just going long on the 30-year, he would be betting that the flattening of the curve will be the result of the price of the 30-year going up. Similarly, if he goes short on the 2-year he is betting that the price of the 2-year will decline.

Cooking Tip: Take both positions, as you do not know which way interest rates will move to make the trade profitable.

Structuring a Yield Curve Trade

As you design a yield curve trade, you need to be aware that discussions of the treasury yield curve take place in yield terms, while treasury futures trade in price terms. In developing a yield curve outlook the first task is to decide how you expect the treasury yield curve to react to interest rate developments during the term of the trade. In general, when yields are falling, the yield curve will steepen. When yields are rising, the yield curve will flatten. These shifts happen because shorter term yields typically respond more to an event like a Fed policy shift than do longer-term yields.

The yield curve slope is simply the difference between the longer term yield and the shorter term yield. Suppose that yields perform as in Table 20.1. Initially, the yield curve is 97 basis points (bps). As 5-year and 10-year treasury cash yields drop 20 bps and 10 bps, respectively, the yield curve steepens by 10 bps to 107 bps. Falling Yields = Steeper Slope.

Table 20.1   Effect of falling yield on yield slope

	Initial yield	Change in yield	Final yield
5-year note	1.99	−20	1.79
10-year note	2.96	−10	2.86
Slope	0.97		1.07

Table 20.2   Price responses to falling yields

	Initial futures price	Change in cash yield (bps)	Final futures price	Difference in futures price
5-year note futures	119.080	−20	120.060	0.300
10-year note futures	123.010	−10	123.050	0.240

Price responses to falling yields are shown in Table 20.2.

The logic of spread trading is straightforward. If you expect the yield curve to steepen, you typically want to buy the spread. If you expect the yield curve to flatten, you will want to sell the spread. You buy or sell a yield curve spread in terms of what you do on the short maturity leg of the trade. If you expect the spread to widen (i.e. to steepen), you can buy the spread by going long on 5-year treasury note futures and short on 10-year treasury note futures. When the yield curve steepens, the 5-year treasury cash yield will fall relative to the 10-year treasury cash yield, and the 5-year note futures price will rise relative to the 10-year note futures price. That is, a long position in 5-year note futures will gain more than a short position in 10-year note futures will lose.

VARIATIONS TO THE RECIPE

More recently a rare opportunity occurred, that is during times of extreme economic turmoil when financial markets experience significant sell-offs. During these periods, investors will sell their equity and lower rated debt investments and buy short-term treasuries. This phenomenon is referred to as a *flight-to-quality*. Short-term treasury prices shoot up, causing a steepening of the yield curve, particularly prominent in the very short end of the curve. Traders will often sell short the short-term treasuries while buying treasuries further out on the curve. The risk with this trade is that it is hard to judge how long it will take for yield spreads to adjust back to more normal levels.

MORE ON THE RECIPE

Because government bonds have no default risk, they represent the risk-free rate of return (though treasury bonds (US) or gilts (UK) are subject to other risks such as interest rate and reinvestment risk). Treasury yields have three components:

1. The risk-free real yield.
2. The *inflation premium* that reflects the expected rate of inflation.

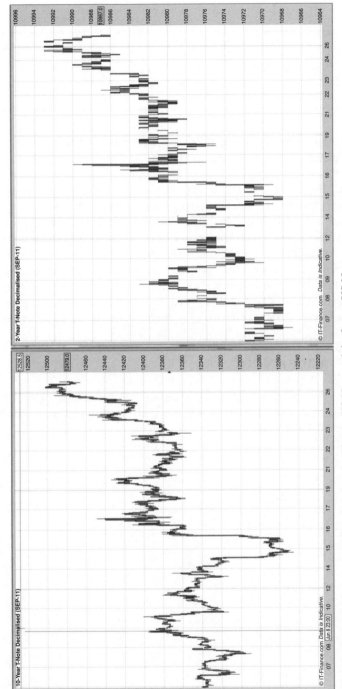

Figure 20.3 Yield curve spread trade using the 10-year US Note and the 2-year US Note

Source: © Sterlingmarkets.com, reproduced with permission

Table 20.3 Profit table for trade

	Initial futures price 15 June	Final futures price 19 June	Difference in futures price
2-year note Sept 2011 futures	−109.70	+109.80	−0.10
10-year note Sept 2011 futures	+122.60	−123.80	1.20

3. The *volatility premium* that represents the risk associated with the price sensitivity of longer maturity bonds to changes in interest rates.

Non-treasury bonds have a fourth component, the credit risk premium, for example corporate bonds issued by a blue chip company could carry such a risk.

A yield curve spread trade is a speculative trade, but it shifts the burden of speculation from taking a position on interest rate or price direction to taking a position on what you expect the yield curve to do. This gives you an extra way to be right, for you have no concern for rate or price direction, only for yield curve steepening or flattening. Further, because spread trades implemented with US treasury futures receive margin credits, this type of strategy can be a low-cost means to capitalise on your yield curve outlook or to defend your portfolio from adverse yield curve shifts.

HERE'S ONE I MADE EARLIER

I purchased the 10-year USA Note at 122.60 and sold the 2-year USA Note at 109.70 at end of day on 15 June 2011. This equated to a view that the yield curve will flatten off. See Figure 20.3 and Table 20.3.

Recipe 21
Buffet: Today's Special at McDonald's
Difficulty Level: Advanced

HISTORY OF THE RECIPE

Did you know that a $10,000 investment in 1965, the year Berkshire Hathaway was taken over by Warren Buffett, was worth $30,000,000 in 2005! This compared to investing in the S&P 500 giving you a total return of $500,000. The 'sage from Omaha' had a mentor and was schooled perfectly into super human proportions by the Ben Graham Center for Value Investing. Buffett perfected this style of investing and he has now become legendary in investment circles, making his investment style the most successful ever. The skill involved in understanding that 50 years from now people will still be buying burgers and drinking coke is merely common sense and that is the main point in everything Buffett does. Apply common sense and if needed wait until you get a chance to buy your stock. If you don't like a stock then simply do not buy it – why bother having the unlimited loss exposure in going short?

In fact, Buffett's not really concerned with the activities of the stock market at all. To paraphrase his famous quote: 'In the short term the market is a popularity contest; in the long term it is a weighing machine'.

The implication is that Buffett does not seek to make a capital gain at all. He wants to ensure that if you pay $100 for an investment, then you will forever get close to $12 interest or in this case dividends each year. This, in simple terms, means that in 10 years the investment has paid for itself and every penny thereafter is profit. Capital gain is a bonus.

INGREDIENTS

When considering a buffet, you need to understand as you walk up to the food counter, that the 'sage from Omaha' does not skip on any of the choices. He will not compromise on quality, and the following questions will help justify your choice:

1. Has the company any debt?
2. Are the earnings consistent and showing an upward trend?
3. Return on equity – is this high?
4. Does the company retain any of its earnings?
5. Is there enough in the bank to maintain current operations?
6. Can the company change its pricing model with changing environment or inflation?
7. How will the company spend its retained earnings?
8. Does the company have an identifiable consumer monopoly?

If we find satisfactory answers to half of these, we will most likely be good investors. To be legendary investors we need to tick all the boxes.

RECIPE

The most involved part of this strategy is ploughing through the company accounts and asking the management pertinent questions so you know that they are a competent bunch. The person who uses scrap paper to make notes is cost conscious, as opposed to the manager who buys expensive stationery. The skill Warren Buffett has is not just in the choice of business, but also an eagle-eyed vision on how good the management is. Unlike some of the other strategies, where we have said you should not fall in love with a stock, here we are more than happy to put money and if necessary more resources towards the growth of a stock. We are fully committed!

Look for a set of principles as this is not as rigid as looking for specific set ups. You need to be more in tune with the company itself and how it may be viewed by the wider public.

1. Invest in quality businesses, not stock symbols.
2. Don't invest for 10 minutes if you're not prepared to invest for 10 years.
3. Scan thousands of stocks looking for a screaming bargain.
4. Calculate how well management is using the money it has.
5. Stay away from 'glitter' stocks.
6. Know what a fat pitch is and what to do with it.
7. Calculate how much money you will make, not whether the stock is undervalued or overvalued according to some academic model.
8. Remove the weeds and water the flowers – not the other way around.
9. Become a conscious investor.

Table 21.1 shows the previous 12 years earnings for Coca-Cola.

Table 21.1   Coca-Cola earnings, 2000–2011

Year	2011	2010	2009
Revenue	$10,517(m)	$35,119(m)	$30,990(m)
EPS	0.82	5.06	2.93
Dividends	0.47	1.76	1.64
Year	2008	2007	2006
Revenue	$31,944(m)	$28,857(m)	$24,088(m)
EPS	2.49	2.57	2.16
Dividends	1.52	1.36	1.24
Year	2005	2004	2003
Revenue	$23,104(m)	$21,962(m)	$21,044(m)
EPS	2.04	2	1.77
Dividends	1.12	1	0.88
Year	2002	2001	2000
Revenue	$19,564(m)	$20,092(m)	$20,458(m)
EPS	1.23	1.6	0.88
Dividends	0.8	0.72	0.68

Warren Buffett currently owns 200,000,000 shares of Coca-Cola making this a 21.6% weighting in his portfolio. The picture above is part of the reason. EPS, i.e. earnings per share, have been growing for years. Dividends are what is paid back to the shareholder. What is interesting is that there are always some earnings retained for the building up of the company asset base through investing this income or buying other brands. Whatever the reason, the second part must be related to the motivations of the management – and what they wish to do with the retained earnings. It is easy to oversimplify this. It is important to know that Buffett recognised more in Coca-Cola than the average investor would do, he knew the minds of the management and understood that the consumer will keep buying this product as long as they are selling Happy Meals at McDonald's.

He will only invest in businesses that he understands, and always insists on a margin of safety. Regarding the types of businesses Berkshire likes to purchase, Buffett stated:

We want businesses

(a) that we can understand;
(b) with favorable long-term prospects;
(c) that are operated by honest and competent people;

and

(d) are available at a very attractive price.

VARIATIONS TO THE RECIPE

The Intelligent Investor by Benjamin Graham is considered by many to be the bible for fundamental analysts. What most people read into this is that you need to have some extra skill set that sets you apart from the crowd. What most people forget is that little bit of common sense. Warren Buffett is always looking at ways to maximise the assets he has not yet invested in. Because there have been no opportunities does not mean we sit tight on cash, as we know inflation will over time erode the value of this cash. So we need to continuously look for ways to put that money to work.

One of the more common strategies is to invest your capital base in government bonds. This does require a healthy bank balance and so is not for everyone. The key here is *value*. We must always seek to add value to our cash, which erodes over time simply because of *inflation*. The best way to create value is through short-term interest rate bonds which pay a greater interest than you will get from just holding cash in the bank. This allows you to abide by the rules of patience waiting for that real jewel of an investment that will pay you 9% to 15% yield on your investment, sustainable over the very long term.

MORE ON THE RECIPE

Warren Buffett originally followed the teachings of his guru, Benjamin Graham. Graham always wanted to know the absolute value of a company, so if a company was trading at $20 and he calculated that it was indeed worth $35, then if the stock ever reached what he called its intrinsic value, he would sell the investment and search for another opportunity. This is where Buffett differed.

Charlie Munger, Buffett's right-hand man, advocated another solution to selling an investment. He argued that if we have bought an excellent business that ticked all the boxes, and the management function was to give priority ONLY to ensuring shareholders' financial gain, then there would NEVER be a reason to sell, UNLESS these circumstances changed. This strategy fully explained why the compounding effect of a business was sustainable, as it was inbred in the fibre of the management as one of their primary goals.

So if you wish to attain similar success, all you need to have is:

- no compromise
- a high rate of return on equity
- an identifiable consumer monopoly
- shareholder-oriented management focus

Using this as your basis, the only other question is then what price do we pay? And herein lies the skill. Price determines your compounded rate of return.

In Buffett's own words:

> At Berkshire's 'World Headquarters' our annual rent is $270,212. More-over, the home-office investment in furniture, art, Coke dispenser, lunch room, high-tech equipment – you name it – totals $301,363. As long as Charlie and I treat your money as if it were our own, Berkshire's managers are likely to be careful with it as well.

Contrast this to ex-Merrill Lynch CEO John Thain, who spent $1.22 million furnishing his personal office in a year Merrill would have gone bankrupt had it not been bought by Bank of America. Watch the pennies and the dollars take care of themselves.

Table 21.2 illustrates what Berkshire Hathaway paid for its investments as of end 2010.

You will notice that there is one holding missing from this list and it does highlight that we are all indeed human. In Buffett's own words to investors: 'As a dividend growth investor, I still consider Procter & Gamble and Johnson & Johnson one of the essential holdings in my dividend stock portfolio'. Warren Buffett is not always right when it comes to selling. He sold his stake in McDonald's in 1998. In his 1998 Letter to Shareholders he mentioned that, 'In particular, my decision to sell McDonald's

Table 21.2 Common stock investments with a market value of more than $1 billion at year end (31/12/2010)

Shares	Company	% of company owned	Cost* (m)	Market (m)
151,610,700	American Express Company	12.6	$ 1,287	46,507
225,000,000	BYD Company, Ltd	9.9	232	1,182
200,000,000	The Coca-Cola Company	8.6	1,299	13,154
29,109,637	ConocoPhillips	2.0	2,028	1,982
45,022,563	Johnson & Johnson	1.6	2,749	2,785
97,214,584	Kraft Foods Inc.	5.6	3,207	3,063
19,259,600	Munich Re	10.5	2,896	2,924
3,947,555	POSCO	4.6	768	1,706
72,391,036	The Procter & Gamble Company	2.6	464	4,657
25,848,838	Sanofi-Aventis	2.0	2,060	1,656
242,163,773	Tesco plc	3.0	1,414	1,608
78,060,769	U.S. Bancorp	4.1	2,401	2,105
39,037,142	Wal-Mart Stores, Inc.	1.1	1,893	2,105
358,936,125	Wells Fargo & Co.	6.8	8,015	11,123
	Others		3,020	4,956
	Total common stocks carried at market		$33,733	$61,513

*This is our actual purchase price and also our tax basis; GAAP 'cost' differs in a few cases because of write-ups ot write-downs that have been required.

was a very big mistake. Overall, you would have been better off last year if I had regularly snuck off to the movies during market hours'.

HERE'S ONE I MADE EARLIER

To bring the concepts discussed together, we will look at Tesco, the UK supermarket chain, with aspirations to become the nemesis to Wal-Mart in the USA.

Let us ask the key questions:

1. Has Tesco consistently performed well?
   (a) They have opened stores in Europe and the USA. They now sell more than just groceries and seem to compete across all retail space, from home furnishings to mobile phones.
   (b) They sell fuel and are bringing the Tesco experience back into the smaller towns by opening smaller stores in high streets.
   (c) Their earnings always seem to beat estimates and are growing – as can be seen from Table 21.3 in 2003 the EPS were for the previous five years growing from 8.12 to 13.54.
2. Does Tesco have any debt issues?
   No.
3. How long has Tesco been around and publicly available to buy on the stock market?
   More than 20 years – so well established.

Table 21.3 Tesco PLC EPS 1998 to 2011

52/3 weeks ended	Turnover (£m)	Profit before tax (£m)	Profit for year (£m)	Basic earnings per share (p)
26 February 2011	67,573	3,535	2,671	33.10
27 February 2010	62,537	3,176	2,336	31.66
28 February 2009	54,300	3,128	2,166	28.92
23 February 2008	47,298	2,803	2,130	26.95
24 February 2007	46,600	2,653	1,899	22.36
25 February 2006	38,300	2,210	1,576	19.70
26 February 2005	33,974	1,962	1,366	17.44
28 February 2004	30,814	1,600	1,100	15.05
22 February 2003	26,337	1,361	946	13.54
23 February 2002	23,653	1,201	830	12.05
24 February 2001	20,988	1,054	767	11.29
26 February 2000	18,796	933	674	10.07
27 February 1999	17,158	842	606	9.14
28 February 1998	16,452	760	532	8.12

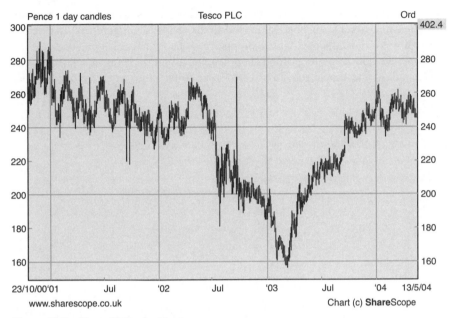

Figure 21.1 Tesco PLC price chart
Source: www.sharescope.co.uk. © ShareScope, reproduced with permission

4. Is the company selling at more than 20% discount to its real value?
   This is the kicker. Finding companies that meet the other criteria is one thing, but determining whether they are undervalued is the most difficult part of value investing, and Buffett's most important skill. To check this, an investor must determine the intrinsic value of a company by analysing a number of business fundamentals, including earnings, revenues and assets. And a company's intrinsic value is usually higher (and more complicated) than its liquidation value – what a company would be worth if it were broken up and sold today. The liquidation value doesn't include intangibles such as the value of a brand name, which is not directly stated on the financial statements.

Once Buffett determines the intrinsic value of the company as a whole, he compares it to its current market capitalisation – the current total worth (price). If his measurement of intrinsic value is at least 25% higher than the company's market capitalisation, Buffett sees the company as one that has value. Sounds easy, doesn't it? Well, Buffett's success, however, depends on his unmatched skill in accurately determining this intrinsic value. While we can outline some of his criteria, we have no way of knowing exactly how he gained such precise mastery of calculating value. What I used was a bit of a cheat, and something that Buffett often mentions. 'Buy!

When everyone is panicking'. The internet bubble was one such event, more recently the financial crisis. For this bit I did resort to the charts, see Figure 21.1 that shows the high was around 290p and it had dropped to 160p.

People are still going to go food shopping and all things being equal, this is one we are still in and should remain invested in up to the point when the overall story changes.

Part VII
DESSERT

It's one thing to know trading recipes, but the most important thing is to understand the errors commonly made even by those with the right strategies. In this part of the book we finesse your skills to make you a more rounded trader.

Life is uncertain, eat dessert first.

—Ernestine Ulmer

Recipe 22
Common Cooking Mistakes and How to Avoid Them

Odds are you know what the odds are.

—Gary Belsky and Thomas Gilovich

What type of trading cook are you? Don't try to be Cordon Bleu if you're really a beans and toast kind of guy. Don't try to fake it with caviar if your palette is more suited to Egg McMuffin. And the best way to determine what type of trading will make you money is to determine your risk appetite. (See you can't get away from the food puns!)

Mistake 1: 'What goes down must come up – especially if I trade commodities or foreign exchange'. Rubbish. Just because something sometimes does, does not mean it always does, and your losses outweigh your profits on the few occasions you were right.

Resolution: Have a stop-loss – a point at which you must exit if you are wrong, as opposed to holding on and letting losses get bigger and bigger in the hope the loss will turn around.

Mistake 2: 'Take profits quickly, ignore the big losses'. This is a stupid mistake because it shows the trader is looking to win a little, and ignoring losing a lot. They are essentially closing exactly the trades which they have accidentally got right and the ones they've got wrong they ignore.

Resolution: Cut losses so that your wins profits outperform your losses total.

Mistake 3: 'A loss is only a paper loss until you take it'. Wrong. Who do you think pays for the loss . . . especially as it gets bigger? The tooth fairy?

Resolution: Take those small losses before you are forced to take big losses.

Mistake 4: 'Count only the winning trades'. This is a popular psychological one. Ignore the losing trades. From this the genius trader works out that they must have something of a winning system as they were right some of the time. Even a monkey with a coin throws heads half the time.

Resolution: Force yourself to examine losses, even more than you do wins.

Mistake 5: 'Have no stop-loss'. Here the trader will let the loss run and run with no plan for when it will end. The reason is either Mistake 1, 2, 3 or 4.

Resolution: Same as above.

Mistake 6: 'No money management'. In other words no idea how you decide how much money to put into a trade. Pick a random number and put that into the trade!

Resolution: You should not lose more than 2% of your trading capital in any one trade.

Mistake 7: 'If only I had held on'. This one is just a variation of Mistake 1 and 5.

Resolution: Cut losses short.

Mistake 8: 'Ahhh ... I learnt what I was doing wrong. I'll get it right now'. This person is constantly looking to shift the goal posts. They always need a bit more money to keep trading – one more fix – as they have now finally got it right and know where they went wrong.

Resolution: Focus on your discipline. If you are not disciplined to follow the rules then get out of the kitchen.

Mistake 9: 'Average down losers'. Here one morning the trader awakens and thinks if I buy even more of the losing trade then the average breakeven point will reduce. It's a sophisticated thought for our simpleton, but wrong. 'Losers average losers'. You are basically tying up even more capital when you've been proven wrong – genius!

Resolution: Don't average down. Simple. The heat is too great and you will get your fingers burnt.

Mistake 10: I need to look for the holy grail. I found another system and another one and another one . . .

Resolution: Stick to the cooking, i.e. keep it simple and execute well. Follow the recipe and don't look for new dishes each time one turns out wrong.

Mistake 11: 'Oh, I made a loss on one trade because XYZ said something about the stock/commodity/currency'. This mistake is, if only the rest of the world would be quiet, I would never have lost any money. And next time I am sure he will keep quiet so I should keep with my faulty system.

Resolution: Excuses, excuses. It's not the kitchen that's the problem, but the cook.

Mistake 12: 'I will short GBP/USD and EUR/USD and Gold'. Here our genius trader does not understand the interconnection between the various securities and that they are actually just doing the identical trade and so risking even more.

Resolution: You wouldn't make three identical dishes and give them three different names would you? Three desserts? No. Diversify. Otherwise you are concentrating your risk by having effectively three times the size of trade you should have.

OTHER INVESTING PROBLEMS AND SOLUTIONS YOU WILL NOT FIND IN THE FINANCIAL PRESS

Sooner or later you will ask yourself whether you should add to a losing stock position. The reasoning will be tempting: 'If it was good at $100, then it must be better at $80'. Such lore is especially popular on online bulletin boards.

But stop. This and other trading myths are costly, yet pervasive – they burrow around in online portals disguised as 'underground investment secrets' awaiting the unwitting. Read what the professional traders say first and it will save you money.

Take 'buying more at a lower price': other variations of this include 'pyramiding'. The idea is that by buying more stock as the price falls, you reduce your average purchase price and so lower your breakeven point.

For instance, if you bought $5,000 of Microsoft stock at $100, then another $5,000 worth when the stock halved in price to $50, the point at which you would breakeven moves from $100 to only $66. It is tempting.

Don't do it. Trading is not about 'getting a win' on any one trade; it is about limiting your losses and maximising your gains over all your trades. If you 'average down' then you're simply less diversified and own twice as much of a company whose price keeps falling. That's fine if you think it is the best place out of 3,000 listed stocks for your money, bad if you just want to 'get a win'.

Moreover, novice investors often confuse price with value. I know my wife does when shopping.

A falling price does not mean a cheaper stock. The value of a stock can be measured by earnings, assets it holds, and other ways. A falling price could reflect simply lower expectations of value.

The investor should instead consider 'in which stock can I best make a return'? It would be great coincidence if the answer is 'the very same one which has been returning me a loss.'

Another favourite among bulletin boardsters is 'pound or dollar cost averaging'. It is a sensible idea but overstated. For example, if you had $12,000 that you wanted to invest in a stock, they would tell you to invest $1,000 per month over a year, rather than investing the whole amount immediately. The rationale is that you will automatically be purchasing more shares when the price is low, and fewer shares when the price is high.

However, since 1950, dollar cost averaging with the S&P 500 has actually failed to beat investing the lump sum at the start of the year in two years out of three.

Of course, cost averaging will win if your start date falls right before a dramatic crash (like October 1987) or at the start of an overall 12-month slump (like most of 2000).

Since we are playing with numbers, there are two further tricks the markets play that are worth remembering.

First is the 'it's down 40%, so it only has to rise 40% to breakeven' mistake. If a stock moves down, say, 40%, then it has to rise more, a whopping 66%, before you are back to breakeven. So think again, the next time someone on a bulletin board argues the stock is 'only down 40%'.

Equally, if the stock moves up 40%, then it only has to move down 28% for you to get all the way back to breakeven. So a 40% rise does not afford you as much protection from a downturn as you might have thought.

I did a straw poll of 25 private investors asking them the answer to the above '40% problems'. Two got the right answers.

The best protection for investors from such myths is through greater financial education at school and on broker sites. A few websites, such as www.practicalmoneyskills.com and www.proshare.org rightly ensure a $5 mistake today does not become a $5,000 mistake tomorrow.

Yet another trick the market plays with numbers is the 'a stock that drops 90% can't go much lower' myth. If a stock drops 90%, you may well reason it does not have further to fall and is worth 'a punt' or worth keeping hold of, or even buying more. Indeed, some investors only look for such stocks.

Well, if a stock is down 90%, you would probably concede that it could easily move down 95%. What is the change in value of your investment if that happens? No, not 5%, but 50%, because if a stock drops 90%, then halves, it is down 95%.

The problem is private investors often make investment decisions on where the price once was ($100), rather than where it is now ($10) which is why they reason, 'surely being down 90%, it does not have much further to go'.

Would you normally be willing to accept a 50% loss? Perversely we are more willing to accept a relatively large loss (50%) if we have already suffered even larger losses (90%).

The professional investor does not think like that. The correct reasoning should be, 'where can I get the best return for the risk I am willing to take at this point; in this investment or some other?'

Sadly, private investors often have a fixation for making back their losses in the same stock in which they incurred them.

Mark Twain had the best advice for the investor who, loaded with market myths, becomes overly confident in his abilities: 'April. This is one of the peculiarly dangerous months to speculate. The others are July, October, December, January, March, May . . .'

Part VIII
PANTRY

Every trader needs to understand the common tools used, whether advanced or beginner. But more than that, traders have to understand the role that risk plays in trading and the psychology of risk. In this section we end the book with some essential words of wisdom borne of our experience and that of others.

> Even the most resourceful housewife cannot create miracles from a rice-less pantry.
>
> —Chinese proverb

Recipe 23
Utensils and Common Ingredients

Over the 35 years, American business has delivered terrific results. It should therefore have been easy for investors to earn juicy returns: All they had to do was piggyback Corporate America in a diversified, low-expense way ... Instead many investors have had experiences ranging from mediocre to disastrous.
　　　　　　　　　　—Warren Buffett (2004 Berkshire Hathaway Annual Report)

Throughout the recipes you will see some common ingredients appearing over and over again. Instead of repeating myself each time, this is what they are, what they're used for and how to source them inexpensively. I've also included the luxury range for those of you with more extravagant tastes.

This chapter is for the beginner in the kitchen. Those who have cooked before can move on.

CHARTING SOFTWARE

Figure 23.1 shows the price moves of USD/GBP using charting software.
　　The key ingredient issues here are:

- Which markets do you plan to trade, e.g. commodities or equities? The greater the number of markets covered by the charting software, then the more expensive it is because of data feed and exchange fees. Thankfully most online brokers nowadays provide the charts and data and you don't need separate expensive software.

Figure 23.2 shows a typical free online broker's chart displaying the price of US dollars to Norwegian krona.

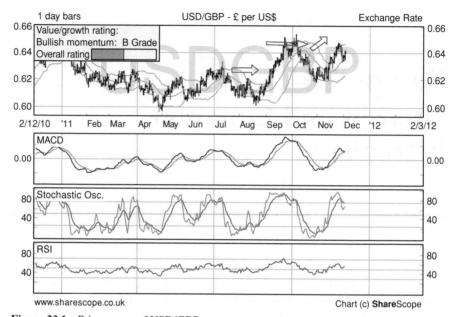

Figure 23.1 Price moves of USD/GBP

Source: www.sharescope.co.uk. © ShareScope, reproduced with permission

- Which time frame? End of day after work or during the day? In which case you may need live by the minute prices, which of course cost more.
- If you plan to use the charts to do complex analytics, then increasingly these are being offered for free on many websites, however, some of the more esoteric stuff is not.
- Web or software? Have you used hotmail (web-based email) and Outlook (software-based email)? Have you noticed the difference? One is dependent on an internet connection making it impossible to work off-line; the other feels more robust and easier to use. It's the same with charting software.

Sourcing inexpensively

Brokers

Many brokers offer free charting packages to their clients. So this is the first place to check. For example www.TradermindMarkets.com offers free intra-day live price charts and analytics.

Web

Forex websites tend to offer forex charting for free.

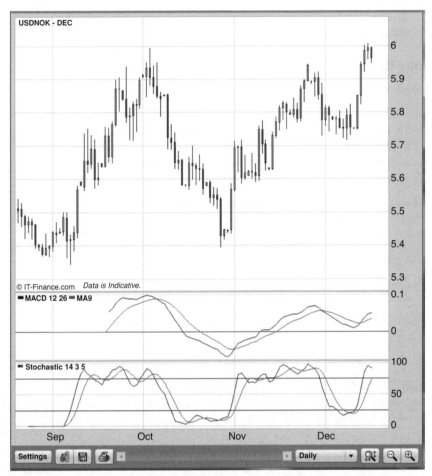

Figure 23.2   Free online broker's chart showing the price of US dollars to Norwegian krona
Source: © Sterlingmarkets.com, reproduced with permission

Other sites such as www.bigcharts.com, Google Finance and MSN Finance offer free charting and analytics.

Software

All of the below software packages offer live intra-day and end-of-day versions and multi-product and geography, e.g. bonds to UK equities. I use Metastock and Sharescope

- ShareScope (www.sharescope.co.uk). I believe this to be the best value.
- E-Signal

- Metastock
- TradeSignal

Luxury Range

Bloomberg

I use Bloomberg (www.bloomberg.com) in my business. However, it is probably not cost efficient if you are only using it for charting, because simpler ingredients will do the job just as effectively, and indeed may better suit your palate and pocket book, since a Bloomberg terminal costs around $1,500 a month.

The benefits:

- Used by professional traders and hedge fund managers.
- George Soros uses Bloomberg!
- It gives you everything you would ever need for every type of trading – ever!

The disadvantages:

- Expensive unless your volume and value of trading covers it.

Figure 23.3 shows an example chart from Bloomberg Professional Service.

Figure 23.3   An example chart from Bloomberg Professional Service

WHAT ALL THOSE CHARTS MEAN

It's a business

Only by treating their trading like a business can private investor traders discover whether they should hang up their mouses. The harsh reality for many is they should.

Start-up costs are the first to consider, including computer costs. Let's assume you spent $1,200 on hardware and that its lifetime is three years; then the cost attributable for one year is $400. Whilst we have put US$ figures here, in our experience in the UK for instance the cost is the same in pounds for most things! I.e. $1,200 of hardware in the US costs £1,200 in the UK.

Running costs also need accounting for. Researching stock picks, even on excellent free sites such as www.vuru.co and www.gurufocus.com, requires internet access.

Flat rate internet access packages will typically cost $150 annually.

Software and data feeds are another running cost. If you use a popular software package add around another $1,000 (about the same in pounds usually by UK providers i.e. £1000) to your annual running cost.

And if you subscribe to an online trading research or tip site add another annual charge of $60.

You will also want some trading books and will probably take a couple of courses so add another $1,000 annually.

Commissions are a major running cost of trading of course – even with discount online brokers. Assume a typical $15 per trade. If you place three trades each week add another $2,340.

So before spreads (the difference between the bid and ask price, representing the amount you would lose if you sold the stock an instant after buying), your total fixed costs (those that don't increase with the trade size) amount to $5,000 annually.

Now, on a $20,000 portfolio that means you require an astounding 25% return annually just to beat those costs. And that's before capital gains tax too.

OHLC bar

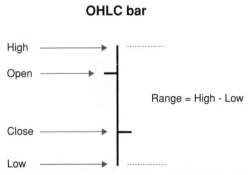

Figure 23.4 Open, high, low, close (OHLC) price bar

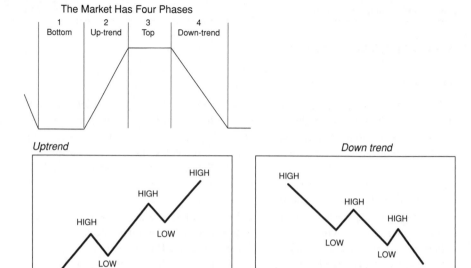

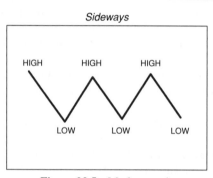

Figure 23.5 Market trends

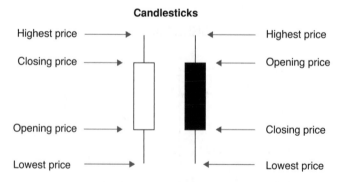

The body is filled if the open is higher than the close.

Figure 23.6 Candlestick charts

Candlesticks Reversal Signals

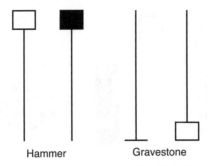

Hammer   Gravestone

Figure 23.7   Patterns in Japanese candlesticks suggesting price reversal

Dark Cloud Cover - Reversal

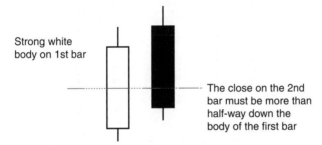

Strong white body on 1st bar

The close on the 2nd bar must be more than half-way down the body of the first bar

Reversal signal after an up-trend

Figure 23.8   Another Japanese candlestick reversal pattern

Morning Star - Reversal

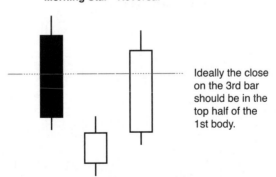

Ideally the close on the 3rd bar should be in the top half of the 1st body.

Figure 23.9   Price reversal pattern – morning star

Evening Star - Reversal

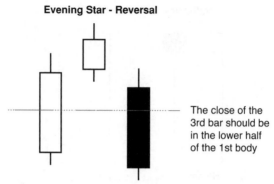

The close of the
3rd bar should be
in the lower half
of the 1st body

Figure 23.10   Price reversal pattern – evening star

Trends

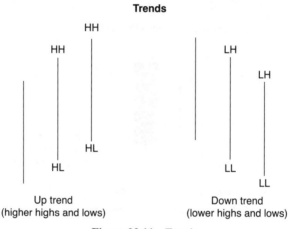

Up trend
(higher highs and lows)

Down trend
(lower highs and lows)

Figure 23.11   Trends

Trends: Start and End

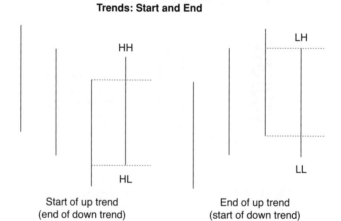

Start of up trend
(end of down trend)

End of up trend
(start of down trend)

Figure 23.12   Trends: start and end

Trading Head and Shoulders

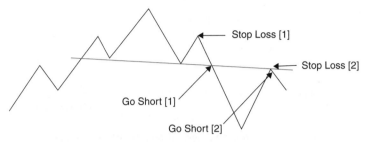

[1] Go short when price breaks below the neck line. Place a stop loss above the last peak. [2] If price rallies back to the neck line, go short on a reversal signal and place a stop loss above the resistance level.

Figure 23.13   A popular price chart pattern

Inverted Head and Shoulders

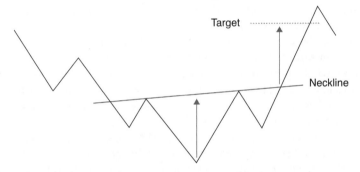

The target is measured vertically from the lowest trough to the neckline (drawn through the peaks on either side). It is then projected upwards from the breakout above the neckline.

Figure 23.14   Inverted head and shoulders pattern

Support Level

The support level is stronger every time that price respects the support line and/or if high volumes are traded at the support level.

Figure 23.15   When TV talking heads talk about 'support'

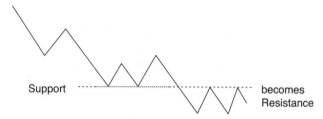

Once penetrated, the support level may act as a resistance
level. Stockholders who bought at the support level will be
inclined to sell when price rallies back to that level, to
recover their losses.

Figure 23.16   Support and resistance

Remember, Warren Buffett only achieves 24% annually on average – and that
made him one of the world's richest men.

If you're not Warren Buffett and expect a more typical 15% average annual return,
then you would still need a $33,000 portfolio to beat these fixed costs.

With a $100,000 portfolio you'd need a more reasonable 5% increase to take care
of the above fixed costs. How many online traders have such a large portfolio?

Clearly, too few online traders have the trading capital to overcome costs and
consequently need improbable returns to make any profit.

Even if you could average a Buffett-like 24% annual return on your $20,000
portfolio, you're still not being well compensated. Imagine that you want to spend six
hours a week researching and monitoring your positions. If you then eke an astounding
$2,000 profit after all costs, you are 'being paid' $6 per hour for your time.

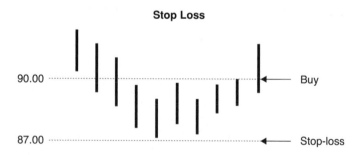

Example of a stop-loss: Stock purchased at $90,00 and
Stop-loss placed at $87.00 (below the recent Low).

Figure 23.17   What analysts mean by a stop-loss

Instead those with smaller sums of capital wishing to increase return on time should change how they trade and consider investing in funds. Even if a fund provides half the return, it will sharply increase your return per hour.

If you want to be self-directed, the catch-22 is that with a large portfolio you could end up losing a lot more in absolute terms and if a novice you are more likely to lose.

The solution? Paper-trade and develop your skills first or trade with a small portfolio, but treat it as a training activity not a profitable one initially.

To increase my returns per hour, I looked for trading systems that produced larger returns from fewer trades. For instance I reduced day-trading futures which involve many trades (and hence a lot of time and increased commissions) to holding positions producing the same returns over a longer trading period (which require close monitoring only when the position is close to exit targets).

Also, like all good businesspeople, remember cutting costs can be a false economy; throwing away those subscriptions and data sites will certainly affect your ability to make returns. Of course, you could always sell your PC to raise online trading capital!

So, one key reason in writing this book is saving time through good strategies generating the returns you need and also suggesting cheap sources of data.

CAN PRIVATE INVESTORS DO IT ANYWAY?

Most definitely yes. The top 100 private investors on www.marketocracy.com have in past years outperformed 99.8% of all US professional fund managers during the second quarter of this year, they also outperformed all the main market indices too.

And these extraordinary online investors are not simply outperforming the professionals by taking excessive risks. www.marketocracy.com requires them to abide by very strict rules.

Firstly, no position can exceed 25% of your total portfolio value. Secondly, half your portfolio must be composed of positions under 5% each. Thirdly, you must classify whether your investment style is growth, value or a blend of the two. This last rule ensures an added professionalism and discipline.

So who are these online investors? Mike is a civil engineer at a water treatment plant. His return in the second quarter of this year was 65%. Michael, a postmaster, achieved 56% and Vladimir, a social scientist, 40%. The Dow rose a paltry 6% over the same period.

Measuring your own portfolio performance isn't straightforward, however. Investors tend to overstate their performance because of mathematical or psychological errors. Mathematical errors include the (in)famous case of the Beardstown Ladies who included cash inflows as part of their returns.

Psychological errors involve rewriting history: 'oh, I had an off day when I picked those two stocks, I'll leave those out of my calculations'.

The maths is a little tricky. Imagine your $1,000 investment grows to $1,500 after three months (i.e. R1 = a 50% gain). You then add another $1,000. The $2,500 then appreciates to \$4,000 over the next nine months (R2 $=$ 60% gain). What is your total return?

$$\text{Total return} = R1 + R2 + R1 \times R2 \text{ or } 0.5 + 0.6 + 0.5 \times 0.6 = 140\%$$

The total return is not simply the profit/capital, i.e. 2,000/2,000 (100%) because your profit was earned on different amounts of capital. For instance, if you produced a 100% return on \$1,000 and then introduced \$10,000 into your account on the last day of the year, your return is still virtually 100%.

Having calculated your performance, how do you beat the fund managers? Exploit the advantages of being small explains Peter Siris in *Guerilla Investing*. That often means small cap investments.

With billions to invest, many funds can't invest even 0.5% of their capital without owning the company outright.

Yet it is small cap stocks that produce higher returns over a long time frame, according to research by Nobel prize winners Merton Miller and Myron Scholes.

Moreover, Ben Warwick in *In Search of Alpha* confirms that with more money under management, pension funds confined to large caps find it increasingly difficult to generate 'alpha' – that is, market-beating returns.

As well as investing in small caps, how else can you beat the fund managers? By adjusting the number of stocks in your portfolio. Robert Hagstrom's *The Warren Buffett Portfolio* explains that a portfolio with 250 stocks is less likely to beat the market than one with 15 stocks. But the fewer the stocks then the more volatile the returns (the beta), i.e. the greater chance you will trail the market too.

Hagstrom suggests Buffett goes for the latter approach: 'put all your eggs in one basket and watch the basket like a hawk'.

If alpha and beta is all Greek to you then of course consider investing through a fund manager, as should those who simply do not have the time or inclination to do their own stock picking. But don't be surprised if your civil engineer neighbour comes home from work in a Ferrari.

SUMMARY

Private investors can and need to cut costs by using the free tools available from online trading websites.

Private investors can and do beat professional traders.

Recipe 24
If You Can't Stand the Heat:
Taking Risks in the Kitchen

> So who still believes markets don't work? Apparently it is only the North Koreans, the Cubans and the active managers.
>
> —Rex Sinquefield

You might need to pursue an aggressive investment strategy but you might also have a conservative stomach. Greater volatility is double-edged: the potential upside is bigger, but the potential downside is also bigger. The issue is where do your preferences lie?

Conservative risk-takers are likely to define risk as potential loss of their principal. Concerned about safety above anything else, they're more willing to accept a lower rate of return in exchange for a lower degree of risk. This may mean that they choose fixed income investment tools such as bonds and may even have a higher percentage of money in their portfolio.

More aggressive risk-takers are less willing to tie up too much money over long periods in low-yielding fixed investments instead preferring the bigger potential returns the riskier stock market may offer.

Of course, your degree of risk tolerance can change over time as you approach certain goals. For example, investors tend to hold on too long to falling stock (risk-loving on downturn) and can sell too quickly on the upside.

TYPES OF TRADER COOKS

Disciplined

This is the ideal type of trader. You take losses and profits with ease. You focus on your system and follow it with discipline. Trading is usually a relaxed activity. You appreciate that a loss does not make for a loser.

Doubter

You find it difficult to execute at signals. You doubt your own abilities. You need to develop self-confidence. Perhaps you should paper trade.

Blamer

All losses are someone else's fault. You blame bad fills, your broker for picking the phone up too slowly, your system for not being perfect. You need to regain your objectivity and self-responsibility.

Victim

Here you blame yourself. You feel the market is out to get you. You start becoming superstitious in your trading.

Optimist

You start thinking, 'It's only money, I'll make it back later'. You think all losses will bounce back to a profit, or that you will start trading properly tomorrow.

Gambler

You are in it for the thrill. Money is a side issue. Risk and reward analysis hardly figures in your trades; you want to be a player: you want the buzz and excitement.

Timid

You enter a trade, but panic at the sight of a profit and take it far too soon. Fear rules your trading.

THE MIND OF A CHEF: HAVE YOU GOT THE MATHS SMARTS?

Here's a spot quiz to measure your trading IQ: you have three doors. Behind one is a car and behind the other two a donkey. You pick, say, door one, and the host, who knows what is behind the other two doors, opens door three, which has a donkey. He then asks if you want to pick door number two. Is it to your advantage to switch?

Most people get the answer wrong, reasoning it makes no difference whether or not you switch your choice. It is in fact beneficial to switch.

What's it got to do with online trading? Everything. The lack of even a rudimentary understanding of probabilities leads to poor trading decisions. It is tests like the one above that investment bankers should use in selecting naturally talented traders, so argues the Centre for the Study of Financial Innovation (CSFI), a London think tank.

If you got the wrong answer, you will be relieved to know there are several online trading sites to assist in calculating the probabilities of success when making an investment.

Handling probabilities is not the only area where your trading IQ may be below par. Reading corporate news is another worrying area. Try this one: you are told that a pack of cards has letters on one side and numbers on the other. Imagine that someone makes the following statement: If there is a vowel on one side then there is an even number on the other. There are four cards drawn, on which A, B, 2, 3 are facing up. Which cards would you need to turn over to decide if the statement is true or false?

A card problem with no relevance to trading? Try telling that to George Soros, the legendary trader. According to him most traders would say A and 2, whereas the correct answer is A and 3.

Most get it wrong because they seek confirmation of a statement, instead of disconfirmation (turning over 2 and finding a vowel would at best only confirm the statement, you need to turn over 3 to disconfirm and disprove it). The ability of traders to look for disconfirmation is rare and profitable argues Soros (see Soros, 1998).

It relates directly to trading because other experiments (e.g. Lopes, 1994) also show that when traders are presented with market news their trading decisions tend to be based on merely confirming their pre-existing views.

The lesson is clear: our trading IQ is improved if in reading financial news sites we look for evidence of our pre-existing views being incorrect. We look for reasons not to buy a stock.

The ability to forecast future price ranges is central to any form of investment. Yet it is another area where traders' IQ appears deficient. For instance, imagine you are asked to make a range prediction such that you are 90% sure that the price of say, Vodafone, will be within that range in 12 months.

The chances are you will be wrong and the price will be outside your range – even though you were asked for 90% certainty. We know traders would get it wrong because research shows over 80% of traders incorrectly forecast the price range of certain equities 12 months hence, even when asked for a range which was so wide they felt 90% sure the price would fall within it (Stephen, 1998). And that's the professionals!

So how can we improve our trading IQ when it comes to price forecasting?

The solution to more accurate forecasting isn't to look at more information about the security whose price you are trying to forecast. More information only boosts your confidence in your ability to make an accurate forecast, not your accuracy (Hilton, 1998). Information is the trading equivalent of Dutch courage.

Armed with our revitalised trading IQ, the next time opportunity knocks on our door, at least we won't make an ass of ourselves – probably.

With trading success there are three key areas, as shown in Figure 24.1.

What if the great online trading boom reduces trader returns and increases the risks taken to achieve them? Well, of the three 'Ms' to trading success (Money management, Mind and Method) it is 'mind' that is the most important. This may sound flaky, but ask professional traders and they will tell you that psychology is more

Trader Vision & Mission: 3M

© 2004 Tradermind™ Limited.

Figure 24.1 Three key areas of trading success
Source: © 2004 Tradermind™ Ltd, reproduced with permission

important than pouring over charts or fiddling with company accounts (to unravel the fiddling the company has already done).

Indeed Harvard, Yale, Stanford, they all run courses on 'Behavioral Finance' where psychology meets money. Yours truly has even lectured about it at Oxford University. And three years ago the Nobel Prize in Economics went for the first time to non-economists; they were psychologists and their subject was the psychology of the markets. So there.

So what are the key mental potholes on the superhighway to trading success?

A report by the CSFI suggests overconfidence is merely one of many psychological 'biases' afflicting traders' performance (Hilton, 1998). Which are the other causes of trader poor performance and what can we do about them?

Confirmation bias is the desire to seek confirmation and resist disconfirmation of one's beliefs. Trading experiments suggest maximum profits go to those few traders who resist confirmation bias by interpreting news dispassionately without a tendency merely to confirm what they already believe. Instead they maintain more of an open mind.

With numerous sites offering stock stories my advice to online traders is that if they are becoming elated at the slightest story which could be interpreted positive for a stock they are holding then they need to step back. Is the story or announcement objectively positive for your holding? The real issue is, how will the market interpret it?

Another way to obtain more objective analysis is to focus on raw stock data. Examine the number of large block trades, market maker demand and stock volume weighted average price, and compare those with other stocks to see if it is relatively positive.

Chat sites reveal the extent of online traders' confirmation bias. Stock holders often reply with abuse to bearish postings. Indeed one columnist, nicknamed Evel

Knievel, who makes bearish stock comments receives abusive email from holders of those stocks.

Optimism bias is another problem that online traders face. It is the tendency to believe one is better than average. For instance studies reveal 95% of drivers believe they are better than average. The CSFI study notes that over-optimistic traders underperform. This bias leads to overconfidence in predictions. Experts are particularly prone to this; expert predictions about financial markets, especially about interest and exchange rates, have been shown in experiments to be generally quite inaccurate and often less accurate than lay views. In one study dustmen were better inflation and GDP predictors than finance ministers (*The Economist*, 1994). This also confirms many online traders' beliefs that they are the best managers of their investments and not 'expert' fund managers.

As traders you must be willing to more readily accept you may be wrong about a stock despite all your online research. Set price levels at which you will accept you were wrong; let the price prove you right or wrong and then act on it.

Another lesson I take from this finding is that we ought to place less reliance on stock 'experts' and their stock picks. I do not know what stocks are going to double next week, no one does. We can only guess probabilities. Experts' pedestals need lowering, they 'know' far less than people think.

Risk aversion biases suggest traders tend to be risk averse when facing a profit and risk loving when facing a loss. Consequently they let their losses run and take their profits prematurely.

I would advise traders with a losing position to consider if they would buy more stock at those price levels. If not, it may be time to sell. Also could you reinvest the money in another stock for potentially better returns? If so, do it rather than falling into the common trap of hoping losing stocks will rebound.

Similarly, when facing a profit, ignore how much you have made or how your other positions are faring. Many traders tend to go for higher risk trades after a string of losses in an attempt to eradicate their past losses, they then take a quick small profit to break their 'losing streak'. Instead remember that your other past and present trades are irrelevant to when you should exit your current stock position.

Herding is yet another fascinating online trader problem. People tend to regret decisions that go wrong more if they were minority decisions. They tend therefore to seek other like-minded people to reinforce their views, perhaps in investment clubs and chat sites. The problem is that the quality of decision is not necessarily improved and can even lead to spurious trade selections, especially if those with contrary views are silenced because of confirmation bias. The key is to do your own research and be confident in it, and not simply because your own view is repeated by others.

Finally, a key skill traders try to develop is to recognise these psychological pitfalls in the market and how they can profit from them. For instance, momentum strategies following price trends can be highly profitable and reliant on a herd mentality of others.

EXERCISES – RISK TOLERANCE

An investor's risk tolerance in making investment decisions can depend on investment goals as well as the investor's personality. The following exercises will measure your reaction to market risk, weight the relative importance of your goals and uncover your personal investment preferences.

Give yourself the points in the brackets for your answer.

1. How much volatility are you willing to accept?
   A. Slight. I do not want to lose money, even if it means my returns are small. (1)
   B. Some. I am willing to accept the occasional loss as long as my money is in sound, high-quality investments that can be expected to grow over time. (3)
   C. Considerable. I am willing to take substantial risk in pursuit of significantly higher returns. (5)
   TOTAL POINTS_____

2. Suppose your investment portfolio contains a significant portion of large company stocks in addition to several other assets. Large company stocks have averaged a compound annual return of 11% over the past 72 years. However, if large company stocks lost 18% of their value in the past year, what would you do?
   A. Sell the large company stock portion of my investment portfolio and realise the loss. (1)
   B. Sell some, but not all, of the large company stock portion (2)
   C. Continue to hold the large company stock portion of my investment portfolio, following a consistent long-term strategy. (3)
   D. Buy more large company stocks. (4)
   TOTAL POINTS_____

3. Please provide your response to the following statement.
   Given my investment time horizon, I am willing to accept significant fluctuations in the value of my investments to achieve potentially higher long-term returns.
   A. Strongly disagree (0)
   B. Disagree (1)
   C. Agree (2)
   D. Strongly agree (5)
   TOTAL POINTS_____

4. Which of the following statements is most true about your risk tolerance and the way you wish to invest to achieve your goal(s)? My investment should . . .
   A. be completely safe; I do not wish to run the risk of losing any principal at any time. (1)
   B. generate regular income that I can spend. (2)
   C. generate some current income and also grow in value over time. (3)

    D. grow over time, but I would also like to generate some current income. (4)

    E. grow substantially in value over time. I do not need to generate current income. (5)

    TOTAL POINTS_____

5. An investor must be prepared to expose his/her investments to increased chances for loss in attempting to achieve higher expected returns. The following statements represent possible outcomes for three hypothetical portfolios at the end of one year. Which investment portfolio would you be most comfortable holding?

    A. Portfolio A has a likely return of 6%, and there is a 10% chance for loss at the end of the year. (2)

    B. Portfolio B has a likely return of 10%, and there is an 18% chance for loss at the end of the year. (3)

    C. Portfolio C has a likely return of 14%, and there is a 25% chance for loss at the end of the year. (4)

    TOTAL POINTS_____

6. I understand the value of my portfolio will fluctuate over time. However, the maximum loss in any one-year period that I am prepared to accept is:

    A. 0% (1)

    B. −5% (2)

    C. −10% (3)

    D. −20% (4)

    E. −30% (5)

    TOTAL POINTS_____

7. Investments in which the principal is '100% safe' sometimes earn less than the inflation rate. This means that, while no money is lost, there is a loss of purchasing power. With respect to your goal(s), which of the following is most true?

    A. My money should be '100% safe,' even if it means my returns do not keep up with inflation. (0)

    B. It is important that the value of my investments keep pace with inflation. I am willing to risk an occasional loss in principal so that my investments may grow at about the same rate as inflation over time. (3)

    C. It is important that my investments grow faster than inflation. I am willing to accept a fair amount of risk to try to achieve this. (5)

    TOTAL POINTS_____

8. Which statement best describes your main concern when selecting an investment?

    A. The potential for loss. (1)

    B. Mostly the potential for loss, but also the potential for gain. (2)

    C. Mostly the potential for gain, but I am still concerned about the potential for loss. (3)

    D. The potential for gain. (4)

    TOTAL POINTS_____

9. Consider the following two investments, A and B. Investment A provides an average annual return of 7% with minimal risk of loss of principal. Investment B provides an average annual return of 10% but carries a potential loss of principal of 20% or more in any one year. If I could choose between Investment A and Investment B to meet my goal(s), I would invest my money:

A. 100% in A and 0% in B (1)

B. 75% in A and 25% in B (2)

C. 50% in A and 50% in B (3)

D. 25% in A and 75% in B (4)

E. 0% in A and 100% in B (5)

TOTAL POINTS_____

If you tended to go for the 'A's and 'B's in the above questions then you are quite averse to risk in your tolerance.

So, if you scored between:

8 and 20 then you tend to be particularly risk averse

21 and 35 then you tend to be neutral towards risk and volatility

36 and 50 then you like market volatility – regarding it as the best opportunity to make money

SUMMARY

Trading success is about knowing how much money to put into a trade so you do not lose too much, even if as expected overall your trading strategy is successful.

Trading success is also dependent on understanding the psychological tricks the mind plays. First be aware of these and then ensure you apply your strategy with discipline so as to overcome them.

REFERENCES

The Economist (1994) April, p. 86.

Hilton, D. (1998) *Psychology and the City.* Number 38, April 1998 (www.csfi.fsnet.co.uk).

Lopes, L.L. (1994) Psychology and economics. *Annual Review of Psychology*, **45**, 197–227.

Soros, G. (1998) *The Crisis of Global Capitalism.* Little Brown.

Stephen, E. (1998) Anchoring and adjustment in economic forecasts. Conference on Judgemental Inputs, University College, London, November.

Index

Index compiled by Terry Halliday